THERE'S A COW
IN MY FREEZER

THE COMPLETE GUIDE TO BUYING, STORING, AND ENJOYING PASTURE-RAISED MEAT IN BULK

Maxine Taylor

There's a Cow in My Freezer; The Complete Guide to Buying, Storing, and Enjoying Pasture-Raised Meat in Bulk.

Copyright © 2020 by Maxine Taylor.

ISBN: 978-0-578-68803-9 (paperback)

This book is also available as an ebook.

Cover design: Maxine Taylor
Author photo: B.K. Phillips Art
Interior design: Matias Baldanza

First printing 2020 / Printed in the United States of America

CONTENTS

PREFACE

When I decided a few years ago to start buying local, pasture-raised meat by the whole (or half or quarter) animal, I expected I'd need to do a little online detective work to find the local farms where I could buy meat this way. What I didn't anticipate were all the other research rabbit holes I ended up falling down. I found myself staying up late learning about heritage livestock breeds, comparing freezer specs, and browsing YouTube videos for organization advice. It seemed like each new tidbit I learned quickly sent me scurrying back to Google with a new question I needed answered or an interesting tangent I wanted to explore. By the time I made my first purchases—a quarter beef, half a lamb, and a quarter hog, all from different farms near my Portland, Oregon, home—my head was full to bursting with all the information I'd learned.

I love researching things ad nauseum, so the three months between the initial idea and the initial purchases were actually quite enjoyable for me. But I know this puts me in a very small minority. I quickly realized that scouring the Internet for all the pieces I needed to put together the puzzle of how people actually buy, store, and use meat in bulk was something that most people wouldn't want or have time to do. The information was out there, but it was scattered; there wasn't a single website, blog, book, or video that clearly and concisely explained everything someone interested in buying meat this way would need and want to know. There was no handy, one-stop source for anyone who didn't have the time, patience, and obsessive tendencies required to find and digest the information piecemeal.

And that lack of a single, all-encompassing resource seemed like a real shame, because the more I researched, the more I realized how workable and worthwhile an option buying local, pasture-raised meat in bulk could be for most people. It's a way to save time and money while getting top-notch nutrition, supporting the local economy, and connecting to a more traditional and ethical way of raising and eating meat. And it isn't just for "country folk" with big houses and big families to feed; single people, apartment dwellers, and urbanites can do this too. So many "regular" people today care about the quality of the meat they eat (humanely raised? grass-fed? organic?) but don't realize there's a better, perfectly feasible option out there besides a weekly stop at the upscale grocery store or farmers market. But without an easy, step-by-step guide to walk them through the process, how many people would actually be willing to take the initial plunge?

The idea to write this book was born out of the simple realization that it was needed. It is a synthesis of my many hours of research and, now, several years of personal experience buying and eating meat this way. It explores why buying local, pasture-raised meat in bulk is such a good idea and provides the practical advice and tools needed to make such purchases easy and stress-free. Whether you're just beginning to entertain the "crazy idea" of buying meat in bulk or have wanted to for awhile but felt overwhelmed or unsure of how to start, it is my sincere hope that this book will give you the information and resources you need to take the next steps forward.

Although I've laid out this book in what I hope is a logical fashion, taking you through the various things you'll need to consider and do in roughly chronological order, it's important to realize that many of the steps in the process can—and, in some cases, should—overlap one another. For example, you'll most likely be looking for the right freezer while also looking for the right farmer, and you'll want to make sure you've figured out how you're going to organize all your meat before it actually arrives. Because of this, I strongly recommend reading through the entire book at least once before embarking on your meat-buying adventure. This way, you'll have a better handle on the big picture and can proceed with confidence, referring back to particular chapters or sections as needed.

CHAPTER 1

WHY BUY LOCAL, PASTURE-RAISED MEAT?

Opinions on what a healthy diet should look like vary widely, and even doctors and health organizations can't agree on a single, optimal meal plan. If you're reading this book, however, you most likely already believe that meat is an important component of human nutrition. You probably already know that meat is an excellent source of protein, zinc, and many other nutrients the body needs, and the only whole-food source of vitamin B12 and heme iron (which is much more bioavailable than the non-heme iron found in plants).

But what you may not realize is that not all meat is created equal (and we're not talking about in a "chicken vs. pork" sort of way). Where your meat comes from and how it's raised have significant and far-reaching impacts. In a number of very real ways, a steak bought at a local farmers market is different—and better—than a steak bought at a big chain grocery store.

What Type of Meat Should You Be Eating?

First things first, what type of meat should you be purchasing and consuming? This is not a question of the superiority of one species over another for health or environmental reasons, but a matter of place and process. Ideally, the meat you eat should come from animals raised on small-scale, family-owned, local farms, rather than a huge, corporation-run feedlot hundreds of miles away. These animals should be raised and killed humanely, subject to as little stress as possible. They should have the space and opportunity to behave the way their genetics have programmed them to behave. They should be fed the food that evolution designed them to eat. In the case of cattle and lambs, this means grass—and only grass. In the case of hogs and poultry, this means a chance to forage on rich pasture with supplemental, high-quality feed. Animals should not be fed or injected with antibiotics or growth hormones. Young animals should be raised with their mothers, allowed to wean naturally.

In short, the meat you eat should come from the type of farm stereotyped in our childhood imaginations, rather than from the industrialized CAFOs (concentrated animal feeding operations) that are the reality of industrialized agriculture.

The Benefits

Eating meat from animals raised in the conditions described above sounds nice, but are there any tangible benefits? A local, ethically sourced pork chop is certainly going to cost more than a pork chop from a standard grocery store, so what justifies paying the higher price? As it turns out, there are many concrete advantages to buying "the good stuff."

It's Better for the Animals' Health

The most immediately obvious advantage of buying this type of meat is that it's clearly better for the animals' health and well-being. In terms of physical health, animals that are not over-crowded in unhygienic conditions and that are fed the diet they evolved to eat are much less likely to contract bacterial, viral, and parasitic infections, which in turn eliminates the need for antibiotics. For example, corn fed to conventionally raised steers acidifies their rumen (the first of four stomach chambers) and disrupts its normal functioning, which causes liver damage and makes the animal more susceptible to life-threatening bloat and infection with bacteria like *E. Coli* and parasites like coccidia. This acidification of the rumen and the subsequent dysfunction and disease it causes doesn't happen when a steer eats only grass.

And while it's impossible to truly know the state of an animal's mental health, conventionally raised livestock experience significantly more stressors than livestock raised on small-scale, ethical farms. Being prematurely and forcibly separated from their mothers, rough handling, overcrowding, transport to new locations, and the inability to practice natural behaviors (for instance, rooting and wallowing for pigs) can all produce significant stress. In fact, this stress can be so high that it causes animal-on-animal aggression. Dehorning, debeaking, and tail docking are commonly performed to prevent injuries, but these procedures are themselves painful and stress-inducing.

The stress an animal experiences, especially immediately before slaughter, can also affect the quality of the meat. After an animal is slaughtered, the glycogen (a storage form of glucose) in muscles is converted to lactic acid, which helps meat retain its pink color, tenderness, and flavor. Adrenaline released by stressed animals causes glycogen stores to be depleted, which means not enough lactic acid is produced after death. This can lead to what is officially known as pale, soft, exudative (PSE) meat or dark, firm, dry (DFD) meat. Both PSE and DFD meat have an undesirable appearance, texture, and flavor and, because of their increased ability to retain water, are more likely to harbor bacteria and spoil sooner.

It's Better for Your Health

Meat from grass-fed and pasture-raised animals is more nutritious than meat from conventionally raised animals. In the case of beef and lamb, grass-fed animals put on significantly less fat than corn-fed ones, and a greater percentage of this fat comes from omega-3s, the beneficial fatty acids that many Americans don't eat enough of relative to the amount of omega-6s they consume. Grass-fed beef and lamb also contain three to five times as much conjugated linoleic acid (CLA), a type of fat with anti-inflammatory properties that's believed to reduce cancer and heart disease risk, as their conventionally raised counterparts. For pastured pork and poultry, total fat content is much closer to, but still usually a bit lower than, the amount of total fat in factory-farmed animals. However, as with grass-fed beef and lamb, the fat of pastured pork and poultry contains a greater percentage of omega-3s. (It's important to understand, however, that none of these animals, regardless of how they're raised and what they're fed, are as significant a source of omega-3s as certain types of seafood, seeds, and nuts.) Thanks to their ability to graze and forage, grass-fed beef and lamb and pasture-raised pork and poultry also contain higher levels of beta carotene (a precursor to vitamin A) and vitamin E, and higher levels of certain minerals, such as selenium.

What *isn't* in pasture-raised meat can also impact human health. While the Food and Drug Administration (FDA) asserts that the animal growth hormones and pesticides (either sprayed directly on the animals or used when growing corn, soy, and other feed ingredients) so heavily used in conventional agriculture do not pose a health risk, many consumers are concerned that these substances can bioaccumulate in the meat—especially in an animal's fat—and cause hormone and immune function disruptions in people who consume the meat. Almost all small-scale farms refrain from using growth hormones and antibiotics, and although pesticides may still be used on pasture land and be present in nonorganic chicken or pig feed, there's a much greater likelihood that these farms follow organic practices, even if they are not officially certified organic. The feed used in commercial poultry operations is also likely to contain an arsenic-based additive (used to hasten growth, improve meat color, and kill parasites) that critics believe can easily bioaccumulate to toxic levels. Feed purchased at local feed stores or made by the farm itself is unlikely to contain arsenic.

It can, however, be difficult to quantify exactly how much healthier grass-fed and pasture-raised meat is compared to meat produced through conventional agriculture. The reason for this is the fact that an animal's meat is only as nutritious as the food it consumes, and unlike conventionally raised animals that are fed a standardized diet to ensure consistency from one feedlot to another, the diets of pastured animals can vary significantly from one small farm to another. The local weather and mineral content of the soil will impact the types and quality of the forage and, by extension, the composition and nutritional content of the meat. Similarly, a pastured pig supplemented with a corn-based feed will have a significantly different meat composition than one supplemented with whey and acorns.

On a larger scale, this type of meat is also far better for public health because it does not contribute to the creation and spread of drug-resistant "superbugs" that can infect both livestock and humans. The FDA estimates that about 80% of the antibiotics used in the United States today are given to conventionally raised livestock animals. Some, such as tetracycline, are given at small, "sub-therapeutic" doses because they improve weight gain. Others are administered in order to combat infections associated with crowded and unsanitary CAFO conditions and feeding corn-based diets to ruminants. The more an antibiotic is used, the more likely pathogens are to become resistant to that particular antibiotic. This means that, in the future, different, stronger drugs must be used against the resistant pathogen, and infections become much more difficult—sometimes impossible—to treat. The Centers for Disease Control and Prevention (CDC) lists antibiotic resistance as one of the most urgent threats to public health today. Because antibiotics and hormones are al-most never given to grass-fed and pastured animals raised on small farms, these operations are not contributing to this ever-worsening public health issue.

It's Better for the Community

The "buy local" movement emphasizes the fact that spending your money at local businesses keeps more of that money circulating in the community. Estimates vary widely, but between 45% and 70% of the money spent at local businesses stays within the local economy, compared to just 15% to 50% of the money spent at businesses that are not locally owned. Choosing to buy meat that was raised on a small farm in your area and butchered locally does more to bolster your city's economy than purchasing meat at a large chain grocery store.

Purchasing this type of meat can also have important ripple effects in the community. Local, independent grocery stores and restaurants often get their meat from nearby farms, and these small farms are more likely to use local banks, often get feed from local suppliers, and may even rent additional grazing land from their neighbors. This interconnectedness means that your support of such farms (and the butchers who process the meat from these farms) helps them maintain and grow their relationships with these other businesses, which prosper in turn. The local raising and processing of meat also helps preserve and even create local jobs.

Buying your meat from small, local farms ensures these farms remain in operation, which preserves farmland that might otherwise be bought and used for other purposes. Small-scale farms are much less disruptive to local ecosystems than industrial, commercial, and even residential developments.

It's Better for the Planet

Buying from small, local farms is also a more environmentally conscientious and sustainable way to eat meat. Because the animals are raised and slaughtered near you, the consumer, smaller quantities of fossil fuels are needed for transport (a concept referred to as "food miles"). Growing and transporting the corn and other grains fed to industrially raised animals requires large amounts of water, fuel, and other resources. By allowing cattle and lambs to graze on local pasture and giving locally produced feed to pigs and chickens, small-scale farms produce meat with a much smaller carbon footprint.

Feedlots and CAFOs pose significant risks to both air and water quality. The high density of animals in a CAFO leads to an enormous amount of waste, which is usually collected into manmade lagoons that can hold tens of millions of gallons of manure. These lagoons emit ammonia, carbon dioxide, methane, hydrogen sulfide, and other gases that are dangerous to human health and contribute to climate change. Hormones, antibiotics, pathogens, and heavy metals present in the manure can leach into groundwater or run off into nearby streams, rivers, and lakes during a heavy rain. In addition, the high concentrations of nitrogen and phosphorous in manure can disrupt aquatic ecosystems and kill fish and other wildlife. By contrast, the relatively small number of animals raised on sustainable, family-run farms produce a manageable amount of waste that can be used effectively on the farm as fertilizer. And, because it's much less likely that these animals have been given antibiotics or hormones or exposed to pesticides and pathogens, their manure is much cleaner than that of animals raised in CAFOs.

Small, local farms are also critical for preserving genetic diversity. When these farms raise traditional (heritage) livestock breeds that might otherwise disappear and use non-GMO feed, they make our food supply more robust and better able to handle disease, natural disasters, and other threats to food security.

Other Benefits

There are other benefits to buying this type of meat that, while less tangible, are no less important. Supporting small, local farms and butcher shops allows you to feel more connected to your food, the people who produce it, and the place where you live. It builds relationships and strengthens communities. Family farms help keep valuable skills and knowledge alive and preserve traditional foodways and cultural heritage.

Buying local, pasture-raised meat is also a way of "putting your money where your morals are." You can't singlehandedly change the industrialized system of agriculture that has become so deeply entrenched in America, but, through your buying habits, you can choose not to support it. You are, in effect, voting with your dollars in favor of a way of farming that prioritizes the health and well-being of animal, human, community, and planet. And, whether you intend them to or not, your actions will serve as an example to friends and family and may encourage them to ask questions, reevaluate where their meat comes from, and possibly even change their own buying habits.

A Final Caveat

It can be easy to automatically equate "local" and "small-scale" with "healthier," "sustainable," "ethical," and all sorts of other positive adjectives. But it's important to remember that this isn't necessarily the case. After all, even the CAFOs of industrialized agriculture (while not selling directly to individual consumers) are local to somewhere. The small-scale farms near you may feed their cattle grain, may not give their chickens adequate room to move around, or may not care about the impact their pigs are having on the local ecosystem. Their soil and the vegetation that grows in it may not be very rich in nutrients. They may administer antibiotics or growth hormones to their animals. While all of these things are very unlikely to be true of local, family-run farms, they are certainly still possible. When selecting a local farm to buy meat from, never make assumptions about the quality of the meat and the integrity of the farmer—do your homework to ensure both product and producer meet the criteria that matter most to you (see Chapter 5 for more information).

Perhaps this chapter has given you new food for thought when it comes to the merits of buying and eating local, pastured meat, or perhaps it simply reiterated information you already knew. Whether you're just beginning to think about the importance of where your meat comes from or have been shopping at farmers markets for years, the goal of this book is the same: to show you that there is a different way to buy this meat—an option that can save you money and time and get you even closer to your food and the people who produce it. In the next chapter, we'll explore what it means to "buy in bulk" and the many benefits of purchasing your meat this way.

CHAPTER 2

WHY BUY MEAT IN BULK?

It's clear that grass-fed and pasture-raised meat has many benefits when compared to meat produced through conventional, industrialized agriculture. What may still be unclear is why you would want to buy large quantities of such meat at one time. After all, why not simply buy meat as you need it at a farmers market or specialty grocery store? Well, for starters, many people live in areas where they don't have access to an upscale supermarket or a local, year-round farmers market. And, as this chapter will explain, even those who do have such resources available to them can enjoy a number of benefits from buying meat in bulk once a year rather than in small quantities on a weekly basis.

Which Meats Can You Buy in Bulk?

This book focuses on the four types of meat most often raised by farmers and sold to consumers in bulk: beef, pork, lamb, and chicken. There are, however, many other meats you may be able to purchase in bulk from local farmers, including duck, turkey, goose, game hen, goat, bison, and elk. Some of these may only be available during the holiday season in November and December. You may also be able to find and purchase locally caught or raised fish (either as fillets or whole fish) and other seafood in bulk.

While this book only discusses beef, pork, lamb, and chicken, the guidance it provides on how bulk meat is priced, purchased, stored, and used can be applied to any species.

What Does It Mean to Buy Meat in Bulk?

When thinking about "buying meat in bulk," the first image that comes to mind for most people is a large package of steaks or chicken thighs bought at Costco or some other wholesale club. But what we're talking about here is buying meat on an even larger scale—buying the entire animal (or at least a portion of it) rather than specific retail cuts.

Meat bought this way has many names—freezer beef, locker beef, rail beef (or lamb, pork, etc.)—but the underlying principle is the same regardless of what it's called: an individual buys a whole or part of an animal (a "share") directly from a farmer and, once that animal is butchered, the buyer receives all the meat from that share, packaged as individual cuts. The buyer usually has a say in some of the butchering specifications, such as whether steaks should be bone-in or deboned, sausage flavors, and the size of roasts. (The origins of the word "freezer" and "locker" should be fairly obvious; the place such large quantities of meat are stored. The term "rail" refers to the rail butchers use to hang meat before it's processed.)

Beef is most often sold as a whole, half ("side"), or quarter. Pork and lamb are usually sold by the whole or half. Chickens (as well as other fowl) are sold whole. Less frequently, you may be able to buy an eighth or even a sixteenth of a steer or a quarter of a hog or lamb. Depending on the farmer and butcher, quarters are sold either as separate front and hind quarters or "mixed." Front and hind quarters contain the cuts only from either the front or rear of the animal, while the more common mixed quarter contains a roughly equal distribution of cuts from both the front and the rear of the animal. When buying meat in bulk, individuals usually also have a chance to receive their share of the animal's organ meats and bones (for their pets or for making stock) if they desire.

When buying meat by the retail cut (at a grocery store, farmers market, etc.), the consumer pays a variable per-pound price based on the perceived desirability of that cut. For example, a ribeye steak might be $13/pound, while ground beef might be only $7/pound. Although meat bought in bulk is packaged into retail cuts, the buyer doesn't pay for those individual cuts. Instead, he or she pays a fixed per-pound price for all the meat in their share. So both the ribeye steak and the ground beef would be, say, $8.50/pound.

How buyers are charged, how to figure out your final per-pound cost, and how much meat you can expect from your share are discussed in detail in Chapter 3.

Advantages of Buying Meat in Bulk

There are a number of advantages to buying meat in such large quantities. Depending on your priorities and unique situation, some benefits may be more important to you than others.

Buying This Way Saves Money and Time

Although buying meat in bulk and a freezer to store it in may be a large upfront investment, it is more economical in the long run than buying the same quality of meat on a weekly basis.

As is the case with many other grocery items, purchasing large quantities of meat at once can provide a significant discount. How much you'll save will vary based on your location, what you purchase, and the farmers and grocery stores you have access to. Buying in bulk directly from a farmer almost certainly won't be cheaper than buying factory-farmed meat at a traditional grocery store, but it will be cheaper than buying a collection of individual cuts from humanely raised animals at a farmers market or from a specialty grocery store.

In exchange for the certainty of a large sale, farmers charge less per pound when someone buys a quarter, half, or whole animal than if they were selling individual cuts piecemeal. Purchasing directly from the farmer also saves money because it cuts out the grocery store as middleman. Retailers must pay their supplier (the farmer), but they also have a number of other expenses—such as store overhead, employee wages, and advertising costs—that are built into the final sticker price of each package of meat they sell.

It's important to keep in mind that when you buy this way, you'll pay a flat rate per pound, regardless of the cut. For example, if you purchase a side of pork and your per-pound price is $5, that price holds true for both the less-expensive cuts (such as ground pork) and the expensive, choice cuts (such as the tenderloin). While $5 may not seem like much of a savings on a pound of ground pork, it is certainly a great deal for a pound of tenderloin.

Having a large amount of meat on hand can also save you money indirectly by reducing how often you eat out or impulse shop at the grocery store. You may also find that having meat on hand saves you time by reducing how often you need to go to the grocery store.

Buying This Way Lessens the Burden of Decision-Making

Purchasing meat in bulk is a powerful decision-making shortcut. Everyone wants to "do the right thing," but sometimes we have difficulty following through. Despite our best intentions, the challenges of daily life can make it hard to stick to the goal of buying locally and ethically raised meat. Perhaps you're too busy to make the trip to the farmers market this week, or maybe it's nearing the end of the month and your budget's stretched thin. Regardless of which stumbling blocks you're most likely to encounter, chances are good that if you have to make your meat-buying decisions on a regular basis, you'll end up with factory-farmed meat more often than you'd like. After all, it's easier to find, cheaper, and the most familiar option.

But by buying all your meat for a year at once, you only have to put forth the effort to make the right choice one time, and then you get to enjoy the results of that choice for months to come.

On a day-to-day basis, having a large stockpile of meat on hand can also help alleviate the pressure of deciding what to make for meals. Rather than going to the grocery store and being confronted by almost endless meal possibilities, you can choose a cut of meat from your freezer and use that as a jumping-off point to construct a meal.

Buying This Way Provides a More Holistic Meat-Eating Experience

When you purchase a quarter, half, or whole animal, you get to sample all the cuts of meat on that animal—not just the popular or choice ones that everyone knows and wants. This is important for two reasons.

First, it ensures that you eat the various cuts in the proportion that nature created them. Everyone loves bacon, but hogs aren't completely made up of bacon. Eating the full range of cuts minimizes waste and helps balance consumption of lean and fatty cuts. Second, being exposed to new and different cuts of meat is a great way to expand your knowledge base and culinary repertoire. In the process of familiarizing yourself with cuts you may have never bought in the past and may not have even heard of before, you're likely to learn more about animal anatomy and discover new recipes, techniques, and cooking traditions.

Buying This Way Provides Peace of Mind

Although the idea of having a freezer full of meat may conjure up negative images of doomsday preppers or off-the-grid survivalists living on the fringes of society, buying meat in bulk can certainly provide a sense of security and self-sufficiency. While having a large supply of quality protein would certainly be useful during a food shortage, certain natural disasters, or periods of civil unrest, it would also be great to have in the (much more likely) event of personal financial troubles. If expenses need to be drastically reduced—for example, because of a job loss—it's comforting to know that an important (and expensive) portion of the household's groceries is already taken care of.

Addressing Potential Concerns About Buying Meat in Bulk

Despite the benefits of buying meat this way, you likely have at least a few concerns that are holding you back. Below are the worries people most often voice when it comes to buying meat in bulk. As you'll see, in many cases these hypothetical problems aren't really problems at all, and instead of needing a solution, all that's required is a shift in mindset.

1. **"The whole idea is just too overwhelming—I don't even know where to start!"**

   As with undertaking anything new and unfamiliar, the process of finding, storing, and using such large quantities of meat can seem very intimidating. You may be able to find some information and resources scattered online, but It's always reassuring to have a comprehensive, step-by-step blueprint to follow. Fortunately, this book provides just that.

2. **"It's too large of an upfront cost."**

   While it's true that buying meat this way does require a considerable amount of on-hand cash (both for the meat itself and a freezer to store it in), there are a number of ways to save the funds needed and techniques for making the process self-sustaining in subsequent years. These budgeting strategies are explored in the next chapter.

3. **"I don't have space for a big freezer."**

   Contrary to what you might expect, you don't need to keep a standalone freezer in a basement, garage, or even a kitchen. This versatility means that even urban apartment dwellers can find a spot for a small-to-medium size freezer. For those extremely short on space, an upright freezer, which has a small footprint, is one option, or you can make your chest freezer do double duty as a "table" for storing lightweight, easy-to-move items. And, once you do the math (see the next chapter), you may discover you need a much smaller freezer than you initially thought. The "Placement" section of Chapter 4 offers guidelines on finding a spot for your freezer.

4. **"I'd be too worried about the power going out and losing everything."**

   If you live in an area with frequent, prolonged power outages, this should be a legitimate concern. However, most city dwellers and suburbanites experience few interruptions in electricity during any given year, and these are usually quite brief (less than a day). You may be surprised to learn that food kept in a standalone freezer will stay frozen solid for between 24 and 72 hours, depending on the type of freezer, how full it is, and the ambient temperature. The power outages you're most likely to experience will last for only a few hours and will have no negative impact on your meat. For more information about what to do in the event of a power outage, see the section "What If Something Goes Wrong?" in Chapter 4.

5. **"My family and I wouldn't be able to eat all that meat before the freezer burn got to it." Or, "I live alone. I could never finish all that meat by myself."**

    Properly packaged meat kept at or below 0° Fahrenheit in a well-maintained freezer will remain free from freezer burn for at least a year, and probably much longer than that. However, you should only purchase the amount of meat your household will consume within about a year; stockpiling anything beyond that can get a bit unwieldy. Determining what that amount would be for your particular situation is a straightforward process, discussed in Chapter 3. If you or your family won't eat much meat in a year, then you can simply use a smaller freezer and order a smaller amount of meat.

6. **"I'd get really tired of eating beef [or pork, lamb, etc.]."**

    The answer to this is simple: either purchase a mix of species for your freezer or, if your yearly meat needs are such that buying multiple species in bulk isn't feasible, you can simply purchase the type of animal you eat most often and then buy individual packages of other meats as needed to add variety. Remember, it doesn't have to be all or nothing—the benefits mentioned above still apply even if only a portion of the meat you consume is purchased in bulk.

7. **"I don't know how to cook all the cuts of meat I would get."**

When you buy meat in bulk, you're likely to end up with cuts you've never cooked before—perhaps some you've never even heard of before. But rather than viewing this as a problem, think of it as a learning opportunity. With the Internet at your fingertips, it's easy to find out everything you ever wanted to know about a particular cut of meat and a dozen different recipes for it within minutes. And, luckily, at its simplest, preparing a particular cut comes down to answering one simple question: Can I cook this fast with high heat, or should I cook it low and slow? For a basic primer on meat cuts and how to prepare them, see Appendices A and B.

8. **"It would take too much effort to actually use what's in the freezer."**

As mentioned above, buying meat in bulk does save time, but maintaining a freezer inventory, meal planning, and actually cooking at home all take a certain amount of forethought and dedication. It's important to be honest with yourself: If, for example, you currently eat out for dinner every day, it would be unrealistic to commit yourself to cooking 100+ pounds of meat at home. If, on the other hand, you already do a lot of cooking at home, the key to making good use of your freezer meat is to create a routine that's easy to stick to. Chapters 7 and 8 provides a number of effective strategies for stream-lining the process of "eating down the freezer."

9. **"My friends and family will think I'm weird." Or, "My children will be horrified and never want to eat meat again."**

While the age-old suggestion to stop caring so much about what other people think of you is still solid advice, in reality it's normal to want those closest to us to approve of our decisions. If friends or family are not supportive, simply educating them on the many benefits of buying meat this way is usually all that's needed (and you know which benefits will speak most to which person). If that isn't enough, making them a delicious meal with some of that meat will almost certainly get them on board.

The concern that children might be too grossed out by the idea of having an entire animal in the freezer to actually eat it suggests that the meat will still be recognizable as a whole animal (worried parents may have visions of an intact carcass crammed into the freezer). But, as explained at the beginning of this chapter, while there may be a whole animal's worth of meat in your freezer, the meat is packaged individually, just as if you'd bought it from a grocery store. For older children, buying meat this way may even give them a deeper appreciation for and interest in the origins of the food they eat.

———

Now that we've examined the "what?" and the "why?" of buying local, pasture-raised meat in bulk, it's time to take a closer look at the "how?" The chapters that follow examine in detail the process of finding, buying, storing, and using large quantities of meat.

CHAPTER 3

FOUR THINGS TO CONSIDER

All big endeavors benefit from a bit of planning beforehand, and buying meat in bulk is no exception. The first step you take in the process should be to spend some time figuring out exactly what—and how much—you'll be buying. This small amount of careful forethought will help you stay on track as you move forward and will minimize the likelihood of future problems (such as discovering you've bought more meat than your freezer can hold).

During this initial planning phase, there are four factors you'll need to consider: budget, space, quantity, and variety. The first two considerations are usually the ones foremost in people's minds, but the latter two are just as critical to making buying in bulk a success. Although everyone's situation is different, one consideration—usually budget or space—often proves to be the limiting factor, impacting decisions made about the other three. It's important, however, to still put careful thought into all four. These considerations should be viewed like pieces of a puzzle, and it's your job to fit them together in the best way possible.

Rather than starting with the factors that are most likely to rein you in, begin by determining the best case scenario. How much and what would you buy if your budget and available space were no object? Once you have this ideal in mind, you can adjust your plans as needed based on the realities of finances and square footage. You may even find that they limit you less than you'd initially feared.

Consideration 1: Quantity – "How Much Meat Should We Buy?"

Ideally, you should purchase enough meat to last your household a year, or six months if you have a large family or little freezer space. (While frozen meat can retain its quality for many months after the one-year mark, the often seasonal nature of raising animals and butchering them means that it's best to aim to make your next purchase of a particular meat at about the same time each year.)

How much meat will your household eat in a year? (Or, more precisely, how much meat will your family eat *at home* in a year?) To get an estimate, simply keep track of the quantity, in pounds, of meat purchased and cooked at home over a two-week period. (Make sure this two-week period represents a typical snapshot of life at your house and doesn't include events that are out of the norm.) Then multiply this amount by 26 to get a ballpark figure for the year. Of course, your household's meat consumption will vary a bit from week to week thanks to holidays and other special occasions, visitors, and trips away from home, but extrapolating a yearly total from a "normal" two-week period should give a close enough figure.

The idea of buying hundreds of pounds of meat at one time might feel like overkill—can your household possibly go through so much meat? But it may surprise you to learn that the average American adult eats somewhere between 200 and 250 pounds of meat per year. Assuming even just half of that amount is eaten at home as opposed to at restaurants, that still amounts to 100–125 pounds of meat per adult annually. Even if your household's projected per-capita total is much lower, it quickly becomes clear how easily "all that meat" will get eaten.

Consideration 2: Variety – "What Types of Meat Should We Buy?"

Next, you need to think about which meat(s) you want to buy— beef, pork, chicken, lamb, etc. This is usually very easy; simply ask yourself what types of meat your household eats most often and likes the most. If the answer isn't immediately obvious, keep track of your meat purchases for a few weeks to see what gets bought most often. You may also want to consider which meats you enjoy cooking and are skilled at preparing. (Grass-fed beef, for example, can be a bit tricky to cook correctly, while pastured pork can be treated the same way in the kitchen as industrially raised pork.) Also consider which meats you're most likely to get tired of (this is especially important if you're feeding picky eaters). Perhaps you want to prioritize certain species because of particular nutritional benefits, such as the high levels of CLA in grass-fed beef.

One important thing to remember is that when you buy a whole or fraction of an animal, you get all the different cuts from that animal, not just the ones you like the most or use most often. You might really enjoy steak, but a quarter beef will only be about 25%–30% steaks; the other 70%–75% will be ground beef, roasts, and stew meat. You may have some great recipes for chicken thighs, but chickens bought in bulk will be whole, not divided into packages of parts like at the grocery store. Before you commit to purchasing a particular meat in bulk, take a look at Appendix A to familiarize yourself with what types of cuts you can expect from that animal.

It may sound trite, but remember that variety is the spice of life. If at all possible, aim to get a mix of at least two different species. The larger selection of cuts this provides will allow you to rotate through a wide array of meals and will prevent the feeling (and taste) of monotony. It's always good to have choices. Ask yourself: in a perfect world, what percentage of your total meat purchase would each species you've decided to purchase constitute?

Figuring Out Quantities for Each Species

Once you know how much total meat you want and what species you'd like to get, you need to make those two factors line up. Unfortunately, this isn't always an easy task. For example, say you've determined you'd like to purchase 160 pounds of meat, with 50% (80 pounds) of it beef, 25% (40 pounds) of it lamb, and the last 25% of it chicken. Unlike buying retail cuts of meat at the grocery store, however, you will likely not be able to break your order into the exact percentages you envision. Because meat sold in bulk is sold by the whole or fraction of an animal, you're constrained by the usual market weights that animals are butchered at. Moreover, since individual animals vary somewhat, you won't know ahead of time exactly, to the pound, how much meat you'll be receiving.

So you'll need to be a bit flexible and allow for some wiggle room. In the example above, the best option would probably be as follows: Order a quarter beef and specify that you would like your share to come from an animal on the small side (many farmers will let you specify a general size preference). You can expect about 90 to 95 pounds of beef from a small quarter. A whole lamb yields about 40 pounds of meat. The remainder of the freezer can be filled with chickens (now accounting for approximately 25 to 30 pounds of meat, rather than the originally desired 40 pounds).

The following chart shows general estimates of how much meat you can expect from the most frequently bought species. The farmer you select may, however, have more precise estimates they can provide you that take into account factors such as the specific breeds raised and what age the farmer prefers to have the animals butchered. Use this information to adjust your ideal mix of meat to one that is workable given the realities of buying in bulk.

Animal	Share Size	Approximate Weight of Take-Home Meat
Beef	Quarter	90–125 pounds
	Half (Side)	180–250 pounds
	Whole	360–500 pounds

Animal	Share Size	Approximate Weight of Take-Home Meat
Pork	Half (Side)	65–85 pounds
	Whole	130–170 pounds
Lamb	Half (Side)	18–22 pounds
	Whole	36–44 pounds
Chicken	Whole	3–7 pounds (includes bones)

What If the Smallest Share of an Animal is Still Too Much?

One problem you may run into is wanting a quantity of a particular meat that's smaller than the smallest "unit" that species is usually sold in. For instance, perhaps you only want (or can only afford or find room for) 30 pounds of pork. This is about one quarter of a hog, but the smallest percentage farmers usually sell hogs at is a half.

If you'd like to take advantage of the lower per-pound prices offered to bulk-meat buyers while minimizing your investment of freezer space and respecting your budgetary constraints and dietary preferences, you have two options. First, you can find a farmer that sells smaller-than-average share sizes, such as an eighth of a steer or a quarter hog. But such farmers may be difficult to find, and the per-pound price for these smaller shares may be significantly higher than the per-pound price for larger share sizes.

The second option is splitting a meat order with someone else (or several people). While a farmer may determine the smallest percentage of an animal he or she is willing to sell to an individual, there's no reason you can't split the meat (and the cost) with other people once the purchase has been made.

But it's important to be selective about who you split the purchase with. Since only one person is officially buying the meat, you'll be putting your trust in the other person to either pay you for their portion (if you make the purchase) or give you the meat that's owed to you (if they make the purchase). The latter concern brings up the delicate issue of equitable division. The number and types of cuts from a share of an animal will never divide perfectly in half (or in thirds, if sharing with two other people). While you can't split a purchase evenly, you should make an effort to split the purchase fairly.

Before you agree to split a purchase with someone, you should have a detailed discussion about who will get what and for how much. Although you won't know ahead of time exactly what you'll be getting, you can use Appendix A as a rough estimate of cuts and quantities to expect. Will you split cuts (and the total cost) as evenly as possible? Does one person want significantly more or less of certain types of cuts? For example, when splitting a half hog, maybe one person wants more bacon and the other wants more pork chops. If that's the case, the weight of each person's portion and the value that the per-pound price represents may be quite different. There's no one-size-fits-all formula for figuring out how much each person should pay based on what they're getting, so it's important to make sure everyone feels like the arrangement is equitable. When you've figured out a plan for sharing the purchase, write it down so that no one forgets what was decided. If you can't come to an agreement about how the meat will be divided and how much each person will pay, don't move forward with the purchase.

As an extreme example, imagine two people are splitting a quarter beef, but Person A only wants the ground beef and Person B will take everything else (the steaks, roasts, and stew meat). Person A will be getting about 30% of the order, while Person B will be getting the other 70%. While they don't know exactly how many pounds the quarter beef will be, they know that the price will be $5/pound hanging weight, with a final price somewhere around $7.25/pound of take-home meat. (The term "hanging weight" will be explained in detail in the section "But How Much Will the Meat Really Cost?" below.) While they could split the bill 30/70, based on the percentage of meat each person is getting, that doesn't seem fair to Person A. After all, $7.25 for a pound of ribeye steak or filet mignon is a much better value than it is for a pound of ground beef. Because of this fact, they decide to split the bill 25/75, which seems fair to both people.

If the other person has never bought meat in bulk before, make sure they fully understand what they're getting into. Do they have, or are they willing to get, a freezer? Do they enjoy meal planning and cooking at home? You may want to lend or buy them a copy of this book to read before you have your discussion.

Some farmers may be able to put you in touch with another customer who's in the same boat as you, but if at all possible only split a purchase with trusted family members or friends—people who you know are responsible and with whom you feel comfortable negotiating and discussing money.

Consideration 3: Space – "How Much Room Do We Have?"

Now that you've determined what and how much you would buy in an ideal world (though one that's still constrained by the way in which bulk meat is sold), it's time to address the first of two big reality checks. You'll need a standalone freezer to store your meat in, and that means you must determine how much freezer you'll require and, more importantly, how much freezer you can comfortably fit into your living space.

How Much Freezer Space Will I Need?

Freezer space is measured in cubic feet of volume. Standalone freezers come in a wide range of capacities, although most people storing meat in bulk will likely purchase one in the 7 to 18 cubic foot range. (For comparison, the average refrigerator freezer is between 3 and 7 cubic feet.)

Freezer-buying guides often suggest that 1 cubic foot of space in a chest freezer will hold approximately 35 pounds of food, while 1 cubic foot of space in an upright freezer will hold approximately 30 pounds of food. (The differences between these two types of freezers will be discussed in depth in the next chapter. Uprights hold less because some of their interior space is taken up by shelving.) It's difficult to say exactly how many pounds will actually fit in a single cubic foot of freezer space because so much depends on the shape of the packages and how they are arranged. Your packages aren't all going to be identically sized rectangles that can be neatly and tightly stacked on top of each other, and whatever organizational system you choose to employ (see Chapter 7) will likely result in the loss of a small amount of freezer real estate.

Because of this uncertainty, and the fact that you won't know ahead of time the *exact* weight of the meat you've purchased, it's better to err on the side of caution when determining what size freezer you'll need. You should estimate 22.5 pounds of food for each cubic foot of chest freezer space and 20 pounds of food for each cubic foot of upright freezer space. So, to calculate what size freezer you'll need, divide your total planned purchase in pounds by either 22.5 (chest) or 20 (upright). Or, alternatively, multiply the cubic feet (which will often be a non-round number such as 8.9 or 12.3) of a particular freezer model you're interested in by either 22.5 or 20 to see if it will be large enough for your needs.

How Much Room Does a Freezer Take Up?

The second, and often more problematic, space-related consideration is how much room can you spare for a freezer of the size you need? If you live in a large house with either a basement or a garage, finding the necessary square footage may not be too difficult. If, however, you live in an apartment or a small house, floorspace is probably at a premium.

First, determine where you'll place the freezer. The next chapter provides additional guidance on freezer placement, and it's important to realize that freezers can be installed almost anywhere where there's a level floor and a nearby electrical outlet. They don't need to be kept only in the "typical" places like garages, basements, and kitchens. You may also want to experiment with moving furniture around to free up more usable floor space. Once you've decided on a location, measure the length and depth of the spot and, if there are potential obstacles overhead such as mounted cabinets, the height. Remember that freezer doors need adequate room to open (either up or out to the side) and you'll need enough space to stand in front of and move things in and out of the freezer. In addition to measuring the area where the freezer will sit, be sure to carefully measure the path that the freezer must take to get there. Pay close attention to tight spots such as doorways, staircases, and sharp hallway turns.

Next, you'll need to take into account the freezer's buffer zone. Freezers need a bit of room on all sides to dissipate the heat they generate. They should have at least four inches of space on each side. Thus, you'll need to subtract eight inches from both your width and depth measurements to find the actual footprint your freezer can occupy. You can then compare these measurements (and the measurements of any tight spaces the freezer will have to fit through) to the dimensions of various freezer models to find one that will fit.

As will be explained in more detail in the next chapter, stand-alone freezers come in two basic shapes: chest freezers are low and have a large footprint, while uprights are tall and have a much smaller footprint. While there are other important issues to consider when deciding between a chest freezer and an upright, if space is in very short supply, you may need to choose an upright.

If you don't have the space to accommodate the size of freezer you would need to hold the quantity of meat you want, you'll need to scale down your meat purchase. Because the total pounds will change, you will also likely need to re-evaluate what size share of each species you'll purchase.

Consideration 4: Budget – "How Much Can We Afford?"

Financial concerns are what most people think of first, because they often impose the greatest limitations, which is why they've been placed last in this chapter. Now that you know how much and what types of meat you would like, and how much space you realistically have, you can finish the process of aligning your ideal with reality by considering how much you can spend. Buying grass-fed and pasture-raised meat in bulk is cheaper than buying it piecemeal from a grocery store or farmers market, but that doesn't mean that it's cheap. Buying meat this way requires you to spend a hefty sum of money up front and then recoup that cost over time.

How Much Will the Meat Cost?

Meat sold in bulk is priced by the pound at a flat rate. To determine how much you'll be spending, simply multiply the per-pound price of meat by the total expected hanging weight of the portion you're purchasing. For example, if you're buying half a lamb at $7.25 a pound and the farmer estimates a half will "hang" at 24 pounds, you can expect to pay $174. Unfortunately, this simple calculation is complicated by the fact that neither you, the farmer, nor the butcher will know exactly how much any specific animal will weigh until after the fact. Thus, your half lamb might weigh anywhere from, say, 21 to 27 pounds, resulting in a total cost ranging between $152.25 and $195.75. Because of this uncertainty, give your budget a cushion of 10% to 15% in case your purchase ends up a bit bigger than expected.

Keep in mind that certain species tend to be costlier—either per pound or in terms of total amount paid—than others. Pork and lamb tend to be more expensive per pound than beef and chicken. And, because steers and hogs are large animals and the smallest fraction of them you can buy is still objectively a lot of meat, beef and pork come with the highest overall price tag.

The per-pound price of meat purchased in bulk can vary significantly from farm to farm, region to region. Even at a single farm, the per-pound price for a whole animal is often slightly less than the per-pound price for a half or quarter. The following chart provides the average per-pound price range for the four most commonly purchased species.

Animal	Per-Pound Hanging Weight Price
Beef	$3.50–$5.50
Pork	$4.50–$6.50
Lamb	$6.00–$8.00
Chicken	$3.50–$5.50

Once you've selected a source for your meat (see Chapter 5), you'll be able to calculate your purchase price more precisely, using the farmer's per-pound price and hanging weight estimate. You should still pad your budget by 10% to 15%, however, in case the animal comes in larger than expected.

If, after totaling all your intended purchases up, the projected cost is more than you can afford, you'll need to make adjustments to your plan. Options include finding cheaper producers, ordering less, and changing the mix of species. See "Finding the Funds" below for suggestions on raising the necessary capital.

But How Much Will the Meat Really Cost?

When buying meat in bulk, it's important to realize that the per-pound price you're charged is not the same as the final per-pound price of the meat you take home. In order to understand why, it's important to first learn a bit of vocabulary.

The "live weight" of an animal, also known as its "weight on the hoof," is how much it weighed right before being slaughtered. The "hanging weight" of the animal is how much it weighs after slaughter, once the head, feet, hide, blood, and internal organs have been removed. The "cut and wrap weight" (also known as "final weight," "boxed weight," "dressed weight," or "take-home weight") is how much meat you actually take home, once it's been sliced and packaged into cuts you'd be able to recognize at a grocery store's meat counter. Discarded bones, connective tissue, and excess fat make up the difference between hanging weight and cut and wrap weight. In the case of beef, moisture lost during the aging process also makes up some of the difference between hanging and cut and wrap weights.

In almost all cases, both farmers and butchers will charge based on the hanging weight of the animal, not the live or cut and wrap weights. Hanging weight is used because cut and wrap weight is variable; there are a number of reasons, unrelated to the sale of the animal itself, that can impact how much meat the buyer takes home. These include whether the buyer chooses bone-in or boneless cuts, how much fat they want trimmed from cuts, and how lean they want their ground meat. Final weight is also dependent on whether or not the buyer chooses to keep the organ meats and other offal—the liver, kidneys, soup bones, pig's feet, etc.

How much weight is "lost" between hanging and cut and wrap? This depends on several factors, including the species, the skill of the butcher, and, as mentioned above, the choices made by the buyer. The chart below provides a rough estimate of the percentage of the hanging weight (the "percentage yield") you can expect to take home as packaged cuts (excluding organ meats and bones).

Animal	Hanging Weight is Approximately...	Final (Take-Home) Weight is Approximately...
Beef	65% of live weight	60% of hanging weight
Pork	70% of live weight	70% of hanging weight
Lamb	50% of live weight	70% of hanging weight

While this way of selling meat has no effect on your total purchase price, it does impact your true per-pound cost. If, when considering your budget, the final per-pound price of the meat you're buying is very important (for example, if you want to ensure you save a certain amount per pound compared to what you pay at the grocery store), then you will need to estimate the per-pound price of the meat you expect to take home. To do this, simply follow this three-step process:

1. Multiply the expected hanging weight by the per-pound price you will be charged. This is the total amount of money you will pay.

2. Multiply the expected hanging weight by the expected percentage yield. This is how much meat you can anticipate taking home.

3. Divide the total price from step 1 by the take-home weight in step 2. This is the true per-pound price.

(You can use the charts provided in this chapter or, if you have a particular farmer already in mind, you can use their exact per-pound price and ask them for a more precise estimate of hanging and final weights based on their personal experience.)

For example, imagine you want to buy a quarter beef. The per-pound hanging weight price is $5.25, and the expected hanging weight is 160 pounds. This means you can expect to pay $840 total. Assuming a 60% yield, you would take home 96 pounds of meat, making the true per-pound price $8.75.

Butchering Fees

In some cases, you will pay the farmer (for raising the meat) and the butcher (for processing the meat) separately. In others, the farmer builds the butcher's fees into the quoted per-pound price—you pay only the farmer, and they take care of paying the butcher on their end. When budgeting and comparing prices between farmers, make sure you are considering the total price, not just the farmer's portion. Farmers' websites should clearly state whether or not the quoted per-pound price is all-inclusive and, if it isn't, the site should provide a breakdown of farmer's fees and butcher's fees.

How much do butchers charge for the work they do? As with the prices charged by farmers, rates can vary significantly and are impacted by factors such as region and species. Generally, the butcher's per-pound price is significantly less than the farmer's per-pound price. Processing fees usually range from $0.50 to $1.00 per pound hanging weight.

In addition to the per-pound cost of processing the meat, butchers often charge a "slaughter fee" or "kill fee." This covers the slaughter of the animal, its transport (if it was killed on the farm), and proper disposal of the carcass after processing. Because kill fees are charged by the animal, you will pay based on your share size. For example, if the kill fee for a steer is $60 and you ordered a quarter, you would pay $15 of the kill fee. Kill fees typically range from $30 to $100 per animal. Even at the same butcher, kill fees usually vary by species: steers are most expensive, followed by hogs, and then lambs.

Butchers may also charge additional fees or higher per-pound prices for special processing of certain cuts. Tenderizing beef, smoking or curing pork, adding flavorings to sausage, and shaping ground meat into patties can increase the total amount charged, although some or all of these services might be included in the standard per-pound butchering fees.

(Chickens, turkeys, and other poultry are often slaughtered and processed on-site by the farmer themselves. Even if the poultry you're buying was processed by a third-party butcher, it's extremely unlikely that you'll have to pay the butcher separately for their services. The slaughter and processing fees—usually $3–$6 per bird, depending on species and size—are almost always folded into the per-pound cost the farmer charges.)

Be sure you understand—and have budgeted for—all butcher's fees associated with processing your purchase before you make it to avoid unpleasant surprises later on.

Buying a Freezer

As discussed above, you'll need a standalone freezer to store your meat. If you happen to already have one, you'll be one step ahead. If not, you'll need to purchase one either new or used. If you can afford it, buying a freezer new is generally recommended, since new freezers come with warranties and are more likely to be energy-efficient and free of problems than older, used models.

The price of a new freezer will of course depend on factors such as size and features. The chart below provides a general estimate of how much you can expect to pay for different types and sizes of freezers at a big-box store like Home Depot or Sears. (These different types of freezers will be discussed in more detail in the next chapter.) Prices at smaller appliance stores tend to be more variable.

Capacity	Chest Freezer	Upright Freezer
5 cu ft	$150–$250	$300–$350 (manual) Automatic models are difficult to find at this size
6 to 9 cu ft	$200–$325	Both manual and automatic models are difficult to find at this size

Capacity	Chest Freezer	Upright Freezer
10 to 13 cu ft	$325–$425	$425–$500 (manual) $475–$550 (automatic)
14 to 20 cu ft	$425–$650	$475–$600 (manual) $550–$850 (automatic)
21 to 25 cu ft	$650–$825	Manual models are difficult to find at this size $900–$1,075 (automatic)

A used freezer can be anywhere from free to almost full retail price, depending on the seller and the condition of the freezer. The "Where and When to Buy" section in the next chapter provides additional guidance on finding and buying used freezers.

There are several other factors besides space and budget that need to be considered when selecting a freezer. Those will be discussed in the next chapter.

Freezer Maintenance Costs

Because a freezer is a large appliance, many people worry that the cost to run it will be substantial. However, modern freezers are extremely energy-efficient, and even the largest models should cost less than $5 a month to run. The chart below lists average annual energy consumption rates in kilowatt hours and the corresponding cost for a variety of freezer sizes and types. In most areas of the United States, the cost of electricity falls somewhere between $0.08/kwh and $0.12/kwh, so a median value of $0.10/kwh has been used.

Capacity	Chest Freezer		Upright Freezer	
	Energy Consumption	Cost to Run (Assuming $0.10/kwh)	Energy Consumption	Cost to Run (Assuming $0.10/kwh)
12 cubic feet and under	225–250 kwh/year	$22.50–$25/year	250–300 kwh/year (manual) 375–425 kwh/year (automatic)	$25–$30/year (manual) $37.50–$42.50/year (automatic)
13 to 16 cubic feet	275–300 kwh/year	$27.50–$30/year	325–400 kwh/year (manual) 425–500 kwh/year (automatic)	$32.50–$40/year (manual) $42.50–$50/year (automatic)
17 cubic feet and above	350–400 kwh/year	$35–$40/year	375–450 kwh/year (manual) 475–550 kwh/year (automatic	$37.50–$45/year (manual) $47.50–$55/year (automatic)

New freezers usually come with a yellow EnergyGuide sheet that indicates how many annual kilowatt hours the freezer is estimated to use based on laboratory testing, as well as an estimate of what this means for your electric bill. It's important to realize that real-world conditions are different from those in a controlled laboratory setting, so actual electricity usage may be a bit higher. If you want a more conservative estimate of upkeep costs, multiply the annual kilowatt hour number given on the EnergyGuide sheet by 1.15 (a 15% buffer) and then multiply that number by your personal electricity rate (for example, if you pay 9.75 cents per kilowatt hour, multiply by 0.0975).

If you plan to buy an older-model used freezer, bear in mind that models built before the early 2000s will be considerably less energy-efficient and could cost much more to run.

Finding the Funds

Yes, buying meat in bulk and a freezer to store it in are expensive big-ticket items. If you're like most people and don't have that sort of money just sitting around, below are several suggestions for raising the capital you need:

- Save over time. If you're willing to wait awhile to make your purchases, you can save a modest amount each month until you have enough. Having a specific goal in mind will increase your motivation to save, and you can even turn it into a game to see how much you can squirrel away each week or month. Small sacrifices such as making coffee at home instead of going to a coffee shop or waiting until the movie you want to see is available to rent rather than taking the entire family to the movie theater can add up surprisingly fast.

- Earmark "extra" money. If you find yourself with money above and beyond your regular income—a tax refund or holiday bonus, for example—consider using this money to pay for your meat and freezer. Just be sure you have the money in hand before making your purchases; don't assume you know how much you'll be getting. For those who get paid biweekly, you may be able to use one of your two third-paycheck-of-the-month paychecks.

- Forego a little luxury. Perhaps you already have money set aside for some other large discretionary purchase that you can use for the meat and freezer instead. Maybe you were planning to take a vacation, redecorate a room, or buy a new camera. Food is a "need," but a freezer full of local, pasture-raised meat is a "want," and only you can decide which of the many "wants" in your life are most important to you and worth spending your money on. Buying a quarter beef might not sound as intrinsically rewarding as a weekend away or a shiny new gadget, but the health benefits and peace of mind it provides may be enough for you to reevaluate what you're spending on.

- Consider buying used. Purchasing your freezer secondhand can potentially save you several hundred dollars. But it's important to only buy a newer-year, energy-efficient model that's in perfect working order from a trusted seller, or your upkeep costs may be significantly higher than mentioned above. For more information, see the "Where and When to Buy" section in the next chapter.

Remember, you should never go into debt or tap into an emergency fund to buy meat in bulk or a freezer to store it.

Making the Process Self-Sustaining

Finding the money to buy meat in bulk for the first time can be a financial challenge, but subsequent purchases don't have to be a shock to your wallet. The good news is that, with a little bit of discipline, it's easy to make the process of buying large quantities of meat once or twice a year a self-sustaining system that won't require you to come up with a large chunk of cash on the spot each time.

The key is to set aside money each month to incrementally save up for next year's purchases. Preferably, this money should be kept in a dedicated savings account (most banks allow you to create and customize the names of sub-accounts) or a secure real-world location so that you're less likely to accidentally—or intentionally—dip into the fund for other things. At the beginning of each month, simply deposit, either electronically or physically, the amount of money you intend to save. Be sure to contribute to your "meat fund" at the beginning of the month (or whenever you get paid) rather than waiting until the end of the month and saving whatever money you happens to have left over.

How much should you be saving? To determine the ideal amount, simply total up your bulk meat purchases and divide by 12 to get a per-month figure. If saving this amount doesn't seem feasible, you can save whatever amount you had been spending per month on meat at the grocery store. To get an accurate idea of how much that is, you'll need to save and review receipts from at least a month's worth of shopping, preferably two or three so that you can get an average. Saving this amount should be doable because it represents no net change in your monthly expenditure. (Depending on what type of meat you were buying before, you may find that the "monthly amount spent on grocery store meat" figure is significantly higher than the "total bulk purchase divided by 12" figure.)

Since farmers and butchers may adjust per-pound prices from year to year, and the exact size of the animals you purchase will vary, the money you've saved might not be enough to completely pay for the next purchase, but it should cover the vast majority of it. And if, in the unlikely event that you decide buying meat this way hasn't worked out well for your household and you won't be purchasing again, at least you will have saved up a nice chunk of change that you can put to some other meaningful use.

———

Now that you've worked your way through these four considerations, you should have a clear idea of how much and what you can realistically find space for and afford. With this roadmap squarely in place, you can move on to the next step in the process—choosing a freezer. The next chapter will help you decide what type of freezer will best meet your needs, when and where to purchase, where to put it, and how to maintain your freezer for maximum efficiency.

CHAPTER 4

CHOOSING A FREEZER

The next step in the process is determining exactly how and where you'll store your meat. Since refrigerator freezers are relatively small, buying in bulk will require you to run a separate freezer. If you happen to already have a standalone freezer that's in good working order, you're set. Most people, however, will need to purchase a freezer specifically to accommodate their bulk meat purchases. When it comes to selecting a freezer, there are three major decisions to make: chest vs. upright, manual vs. automatic defrost, and size.

Decision 1: Chest vs. Upright Freezer

Standalone freezers come in two varieties: chest and upright. Chest freezers sit relatively low to the ground and open from the top. They may have one or two hanging baskets, and fancier models may contain vertical dividers, but they are basically just a large insulated box. Upright freezers look similar to refrigerators—they're tall, have shelves, and open from the front.

Chest freezers offer many advantages. When compared to an upright freezer of the same size, they cost less and are cheaper to operate because they're more energy-efficient. They offer more usable space thanks to their open, shelf-free design. And, since their door is located at the top and cold air sinks, chest freezers will keep their contents cold longer than an upright in the event of a power outage.

Chest freezers, however, have two main disadvantages. First, because of their top-load design and lack of shelves, they can be very challenging to organize. Without some sort of system in place, it can become time consuming to dig through a full chest freezer to find a particular item. Second, chest freezers have a much larger footprint than upright freezers of the same cubic footage. This may make it more difficult to find a place to keep a chest freezer, especially if keeping it in a garage or basement is not an option. This particular drawback is somewhat mitigated by the fact that you can store things on top of a chest freezer, making it a sort of table (although of course these items will need to be moved every time you open the freezer).

On the other hand, the shelves and front-facing door of an upright freezer make it much easier to organize and access food. Their design also makes them easier to clean than chest freezers, since much less bending over is required. Uprights also take up much less floor space, which can be a major advantage if square footage is limited. Uprights also tend to come in more color and finish options. But uprights have several key drawbacks. In addition to being more expensive to purchase and operate than comparably sized chest freezers, the design of upright freezers allows more cold air to escape even if the door seal is tight, which means they are less effective in maintaining their temperature during a power outage. And if you're looking for a freezer under

10 cubic feet, you'll find far fewer upright options compared to chest freezers.

Decision 2: Manual vs. Automatic Defrost

The second key choice you'll need to make when selecting a freezer is how to deal with frost buildup. A thick layer of frost inside a freezer will prevent the freezer's cooling apparatus (a series of gas-filled pipes located within the walls of the freezer) from working efficiently. The frost acts as an insulator, preventing the cold generated by the pipes from transferring to the interior of the freezer, where the food is, forcing the freezer to work harder to keep the contents of the freezer at the specified temperature. Therefore, it's important to keep your freezer as free of frost as possible. Defrosting can either be done manually or automatically.

Manually defrosting a freezer involves emptying it, unplugging it, and allowing the accumulated frost to melt into water, which is then drained through an opening at the bottom of the freezer. Automatic (frost-free) freezers work by occasionally raising the temperature inside the freezer to just above freezing for a short period of time. This causes any accumulated frost to melt, and it then drains to an external tray that sits above the freezer's heat exchange, which helps evaporate the water. Chest freezers are always manual; upright freezers may be either manual or automatic.

Automatic freezers are obviously much more convenient than manual freezers. Having to unplug the freezer for a day or so to manually defrost it presents a major logistical problem:

the freezer either needs to be empty or you'll need a place to temporarily store your food. It's likely that you won't have completely depleted your stockpile of meat before purchasing more, so it may be challenging to find a time when the freezer is empty enough to manually defrost.

In all other respects, however, manual freezers are superior to automatic freezers. They offer better food preservation because the temperature within the freezer always stays below freezing. Frost-free freezers must run their compressor to temporarily warm the air inside, and the increased use of the compressor means that automatic freezers are louder and use more energy (and thus cost more to run). Manual freezers are also cheaper than automatic freezers of the same size.

A manual freezer should be defrosted once the ice layer has reached a quarter of an inch thick. How quickly the frost builds up to that thickness will depend on a number of factors. To minimize frost buildup, place the freezer away from major heat sources, keep the freezer full (using jugs of frozen water if necessary), do not place unfrozen food directly into your standalone freezer (freeze it in your refrigerator freezer first), minimize the amount of time the freezer door is open, and make sure the door seals tightly.

Always take the opportunity to defrost your freezer if it becomes empty, or empty enough to transfer the remaining contents to your refrigerator freezer or a cooler with ice. An easy way to deal with frost buildup before it becomes a problem, however, is to periodically scrape the sides of the freezer with a flat plastic dish scraper. Remove the contents of the freezer (they will only be out for a few minutes, so there's no need to worry about them thawing) and use the edge of the scraper to dislodge frost, which can be caught in a small pan or other container and disposed of. Never use a metal object to scrape the sides of the freezer. By using this method and following the suggestions above, you may not ever need to fully defrost a manual freezer.

Decision 3: Size

Lastly, you'll need to decide what size freezer to buy. In the previous chapter, you determined how many cubic feet you need to store the amount of meat you're planning to purchase, given any budgetary and space constraints. This number, however, should be considered a minimum. Once they have a standalone freezer for meat bought in bulk, most people find that they have many other things they'd like to store there as well. So it's generally a good idea to purchase the largest freezer that you can comfortably afford and make room for. For example, you may only need 7 cubic feet of space for the meat you've purchased, but the extra capacity provided by a 9-cubic-foot freezer will allow you to stock up when your favorite grocery store items are on sale, cook and freeze homemade meals in large batches, and preserve produce from your garden or the farmers market. And, if you find you aren't using the extra space, it can always be filled with ice or frozen jugs of water, which can be handy in an emergency.

Special Features

Both upright and chest freezers are relatively simple appliances with few bells and whistles. There are, however, a few features you may want to have. These include:

External Power Indicator Light: Most newer freezer models have an external power light to let you know they're running. While this is a useful feature, it's important to note that in as little as a year or two, many power lights begin flickering or may go out completely, even though the freezer itself still works fine.

Digital Temperature Control: Most freezers have a manual temperature control dial with rather imprecise "cold/colder/coldest" markings Some higher-end freezers, however, use a digital thermostat that allows you to easily see and precisely control the temperature in the freezer.

Organization Options: The shelves of an upright freezer may be adjustable rather than fixed, allowing for greater ability to customize its organization. Small chest freezers usually come with only one hanging basket to organize small items, while larger models may come with two or even three. Some chest freezers also come with removable plastic dividers to help divide the large area inside into more manageable spaces. While such dividers can be helpful, they take up valuable space themselves and may not divide the freezer in a way that's useful for you.

Lock: Some freezers (usually chest freezers) have locking lids. This can prevent small children from accidentally climbing in and becoming trapped inside. The ability to lock the freezer may also come in handy if you are living in a shared space and want an extra level of security.

Interior Light: Having a small light inside the freezer can make it easier to find specific items. Such lights are much more common in uprights.

Temperature Alarm: A temperature alarm will alert you if the temperature inside the freezer rises above a certain point. Although such a warning system is useful in the case of a mechanical failure, it will most likely not be operational in the case of a power outage.

Soft Freeze Zone: Some frost-free uprights have a "soft freeze zone"—an area of the freezer usually located on the door where you can keep items you don't want to freeze hard, such as ice cream. If you're using your standalone freezer primarily for meat storage, however, such a feature is not very useful.

What About the Brand?

There are many brands of freezer available, but only three main freezer manufacturers. In addition to selling freezers under its own name, Frigidaire manufactures the Kelvinator brand and some Kenmore and GE models. W.C. Wood makes Danby and Whirlpool brands, as well as some Amana and Maytag models. Haier makes some Kenmore, GE, Maytag, and Amana models, as well as its own line of freezers. Because almost all freezers come from one of these three manufacturers, there is very little difference from one brand to another.

If you feel loyalty toward a particular brand, you can certainly take that into account when picking a freezer. If you don't have a personal preference for brand, simply go with whatever model fits your requirements, has the features you want, and is at the right price. As with any other big purchase, it can be helpful to read reviews online. If you have a subscription to *Consumer Reports*, this can be a good place to start. Also check customer reviews on a number of retailer websites (such as Amazon, Sears, and Home Depot), regardless of whether or not you plan to purchase from those retailers. You may also want to compare freezers' energy efficiency on the Energy Star website.

Where and When to Buy

Standalone freezers can be purchased new from local appliance shops as well as national chain appliance retailers (such as Sears) and home improvement stores (such as Lowe's and Home Depot). They can also be purchased at online-only retailers like Amazon. Shipping charges, however, may be prohibitively expensive, and it's always nice to be able to see the freezer in person before buying. Seeing the freezer in person allows you to check small but important details (like cord placement and length) that aren't usually noted in product descriptions but can have a major impact on where you place the freezer. You may want to look at a particular model in person at one retailer and then order it online for in-store pickup or home delivery from another retailer selling it at a lower price.

Freezers can also be purchased used at garage and estate sales; on sites like Craigslist, Ebay, Nextdoor, and Facebook Marketplace; and at local used appliance stores. If buying used, make absolutely sure the freezer runs before buying it, and keep in mind that older models may be less efficient than newer ones. Be sure to thoroughly clean the inside and outside of the freezer, even if it appears clean.

If purchasing new or used from a retailer, remember to ask about their refund policy and any additional warranties they offer. If purchasing a secondhand model, use the freezer's model number (usually located on its back panel) to find the user's manual online. In addition to providing information about using and caring for the freezer, it will also outline the conditions of the manufacturer's warranty.

Unlike with major appliances such as ovens and dishwashers, there are rarely big sales on standalone freezers, especially those under 15 cubic feet. Standalone freezers aren't updated as often as other appliances, so stores rarely need to get rid of old inventory to make room for new stock. That being said, you may be able to find slightly better deals at certain times of the year. These include May (when new refrigerator models are usually revealed), September and October (when new models of most other appliances are rolled out), the end of each month and calendar quarter (when retailers are working hard to meet sales quotas), and during holiday weekends (when retailers are more likely to have special storewide sales and promotions). As with any large purchase, it's always a good idea to search for store coupons, rebates, free delivery deals, and other discounts.

Make sure you have your freezer at least a week or two before your meat is ready. This will give you some wiggle room in case there are any problems. (Keep in mind that the freezer may not be ready for pick-up or delivery immediately after purchase. Be sure to allow extra time for this possible delay.) Once you have the freezer (and any time it's moved in the future), let it sit, unplugged, for 24 hours. This allows any compressor oil that may have leaked during transport to settle and will prevent your freezer from potentially malfunctioning. After the freezer has rested, plug it in to make sure it works. You can then leave it unplugged until it's ready to be filled.

Placement

While most people place their standalone freezer in either a garage or basement, these are certainly not your only options. In fact, having the freezer in your main living space can help serve as a visual reminder to use its contents. And, in the unlikely event that the freezer stops working, you'll notice sooner if you walk past it multiple times a day. Kitchens, dining rooms, living rooms, and spare bedrooms are all viable options if space and aesthetics allow. Just like a refrigerator, standalone freezers emit only a quiet hum when the compressor or circulating fans are running (and make no noise at all when they aren't), so the freezer should cause little if any distraction. Freezers run on the standard household current of 120 volts, so any wall outlet with a ground can be used.

Placing a freezer on low-pile (non-shag) carpet is safe, although it's advisable to lay down a thin sheet of plywood first to add an extra layer of protection and prevent the freezer's feet from creating crush spots in the carpeting. You'll also need to use a bit of extra caution when manually defrosting a freezer that's placed on carpet. The freezer should have at least four inches of space on all sides to allow the heat it generates to dissipate. Keep freezers away from heat sources like stoves, hot water heaters, and sunny windows. Never use an extension cord or plug a freezer into a power strip. Ensure that the freezer is level (most freezers have adjustable feet, or you can also use thin wooden shims to ensure levelness).

Achieving Maximum Efficiency

Freezers are never as energy-efficient as they claim, since the laboratory settings in which they're tested are not the same as the real world. That being said, freezers use very little energy and there are a number of things you can do to maximize their efficiency.

How full a freezer is has a major impact on its efficiency. For best results, a freezer should be kept at least two-thirds full at all times. If there isn't enough meat in your freezer to reach this mark, you can add bags of ice or frozen jugs of water to fill the extra space. Never fill a freezer so full that the door cannot be firmly shut.

The temperature of the food you add to the freezer also plays a significant role in its efficiency. Your bulk meat purchase will be already frozen when you pick it up, but if you're going to add any additional food to your freezer (such as leftovers, surplus from your garden, or stock-up items purchased at a grocery store), make sure it has already been pre-frozen in your refrigerator freezer or, at the very least, cooled completely in the fridge.

Minimizing the number of times you open the freezer, and how long the freezer stays open each time, will also decrease energy consumption. Following a meal plan (see Chapter 8) can cut down on how often you need to open the freezer; you can take everything you need for the next week's meals out at once and move it to either the refrigerator or refrigerator freezer.

Having a well-organized freezer and using an inventory list will also make it much quicker to find what you're looking for (see Chapter 7).

Be sure to periodically check the rubber gasket around the freezer lid to make sure it's clean and undamaged; an improperly sealing lid will require the freezer to work harder to keep its contents at the ideal temperature (0° Fahrenheit or below). And, as mentioned above, place your freezer away from heat sources and keep it as frost-free as possible.

If you suspect your freezer is using significantly more power than it should (because your electric bill is high or the compressor is running constantly), you may want to purchase an energy usage meter such as the Kill a Watt. This device measures how much electricity a particular device or appliance is using and can extrapolate out how much it will use over a week, month, or year—and how much that power consumption will cost.

Upkeep

In general, standalone freezers require very little maintenance. In addition to periodic frost scraping (if using a chest freezer or a manual upright freezer), you'll want to occasionally wipe down the freezer's exterior and door gaskets to keep them free of dust. Depending on the model of freezer you're using, you may also be able to easily access the freezer's condenser coils and fans. If so, these should periodically be vacuumed to remove dust build-up. Your user's manual will provide detailed instructions on how this can be done, as well as any other necessary maintenance tasks. With just this minimal amount of care, a freezer should last many, many years.

What If Something Goes Wrong?

Undoubtedly everyone's biggest fear when purchasing large quantities of meat for long-term storage is what happens if the power goes out or the freezer breaks? The idea of losing hundreds of dollars' worth of food is anxiety-inducing, but there are a few things you can do if the freezer isn't operational to minimize the potential for disaster.

It should almost go without saying that in the event of a power outage or mechanical failure, the freezer should be opened as little as possible. If the freezer isn't running, you should only open it to move items to a safer location or to add ice to help keep the contents frozen. Dry ice, however, can "burn" meat through packaging and should not be used. Fully cover the top and all four sides of the freezer with heavy blankets to keep it as insulated as possible. (The freezer should never be covered like this while it's running, since this will prevent heat from dissipating.)

Standalone freezers are quite simple and are known for being very reliable. If a mechanical failure does occur, the most important thing is that you notice it as soon as possible. Because standalone freezers (especially manual defrost models) are often totally silent for hours at a time, simply listening for a hum is not an effective way to know if the freezer is operating smoothly. An external power indicator light or temperature alarm can be very useful, but even if your freezer has these features it's still a good idea to quickly check the contents of the freezer every few days.

(And, as mentioned earlier, power indicator lights often malfunction, despite the freezer itself working perfectly.)

Should a problem occur, call the retailer from which you bought the freezer or an appliance repair company immediately. If possible, move as much of the freezer's contents to your refrigerator freezer, coolers, and/or friends' and family's freezers. Many freezers come with a warranty that protects against food loss in the event of a mechanical failure.

Assuming the ambient temperature is not inordinately hot, an unopened, full upright freezer without power or experiencing a malfunction will keep food fully frozen for at least 24 hours, and an unopened, full chest freezer will keep its contents frozen for at least 48 to 72 hours. Still, if you live in an area prone to extended power outages, you may need to invest in a generator to run your standalone freezer and other essential appliances.

———

Once your freezer is up and running, it's important to keep its contents well organized. Having a system in place will reduce frustration when looking for a specific item and will make the whole process of using the meat you've bought more enjoyable. Strategies for organizing your freezer will be discussed in Chapter 7.

CHAPTER 5

SELECTING A FARMER

You now know what (and how much) meat you want, but where do you find it? This is a two-step task that involves first locating potential suppliers (farmers) and then evaluating them against one another to determine which is best able to meet your needs. This part of the buying process can be a bit time-consuming sometimes, but it shouldn't be rushed. Ideally, taking the time and effort to choose carefully now will mean that you'll only have to make this decision once: after you find a farmer who's easy to work with and provides a product you love, you can buy from them year after year.

Where to Look

People living in a more rural area likely have a general idea of how many farms exist nearby, but many big city dwellers may have the impression that finding a local farmer to buy from will be difficult. In fact, the opposite is usually true: there are often numerous small-scale, family-run farms within a 50-mile radius of large metropolitan areas, simply because the high concentration of people there makes for a large and convenient customer base. Although the farms themselves may not have high visibility, urbanites can likely find their products at farmers markets, farm-to-table restaurants, and high-end local grocery stores and specialty meat markets.

Below are six places to begin your search for local, pastured-raised meat:

Eatwild. Founded by Jo Robinson in 2001, Eatwild (www. eatwild.com) has grown to become the most comprehensive online source for information on the many benefits of eating local, pasture-raised meat and animal products. Their site includes an extensive state-by-state listing of small-scale meat, dairy, and egg producers, with descriptions of each farm's offerings as well as website and contact information. Although the site doesn't catalog all available options (likely because farmers must apply and pay an annual listing fee) and some listings may be out of date, this is still the best places to begin your search.

LocalHarvest. The mission of LocalHarvest (www. localharvest.org) is to "connect people looking for good food with the farmers who produce it." To that end, this site lists much more than just local meat producers; it also includes listings for local fruit/vegetable farms, CSAs, farmers markets, and sustainable restaurants and grocery stores. You can narrow your search by city or zip code and filter for only "farms," although you may still need to look through many listings to find farms that sell meat in bulk direct to consumers.

Farmers markets. Search for farmers markets in your town or city, as well as those in nearby locations. Most markets will have a website that lists their vendors. In addition to those selling meat, take note of any offering dairy or eggs, since they may also raise meat animals but choose not to sell them at the farmers market. If the farmers market vendors you find don't have websites of their own, search for an email address, Facebook page, or phone number through which to contact each farm for additional information. Even if they don't offer what you're looking for, they may know another farmer who does.

Google. Never underestimate the power of a simple web search. Use a combination of keywords such as "bulk," "grass-fed," "pasture-raised," and "pastured"; the word "meat" or the specific meats you're looking for (beef, pork, lamb, etc.); and your zip code, town/city/county name, or the name of the nearest large city. Good phrases to use include "grass-fed beef near [your location]," "pasture-raised meat near me," "bulk pork in [your state]," etc. Scan through the first two or three pages of search results for applicable farms.

Recommendations. If you know of any local friends, family members, or coworkers who have purchased meat in bulk before, you should of course ask them for their suggestions and opinions. In fact, if you're fortunate enough to know someone near you who has bought meat this way before, they should be your very first point of contact when conducting your search. If you don't know anyone personally who you can ask, you can solicit recommendations from users on community groups like Nextdoor and city-specific Reddit forums.

Local High-End Grocery Stores, Butchers, Meat Markets, and Farm-to-Table Restaurants. If your town or city happens to have a local grocer, retail butcher, meat market, or restaurant that advertises itself as "farm-to-table" or "farm-to-fork," ask them where their meat comes from. If it's sourced from nearby farms, you may be able to purchase a share of an animal directly from the supplier.

Selection Criteria

Contrary to what you might have expected, you'll most likely end up with a number of farmers to choose between. To decide who you'll eventually purchase from, you'll need to figure out what matters most to you and then see how each candidate compares. There are a number of criteria you may want to consider, and top priorities will vary significantly from person to person. For example, one individual may want meat that's certified organic, while another may not care about this at all but wants to find a farmer less than 15 miles from home.

Create a chart with the criteria that are most important to you in rows along the left-hand side and the potential farmers you're considering in columns across the top. Be sure to include each farmer's website, phone number, email, and address directly under their name for easy reference. You will also want to include the name and contact information of the butcher the farmer uses, since some factors you may be considering might relate to the processing, rather than the raising, of the meat. (Appendix C provides a template you can use as the basis for your own chart.) Then begin filling out the chart. You can usually get much of the information you're looking for on the farmer's website, but to fill in all the details (or if the farmer doesn't have a web presence), you will need to call or email for more information. Be sure to include a "Notes" row where you can keep track of the last time you called or emailed, as it may get difficult to keep track of where you are in the process with each candidate. This is also a good place to put any additional information that might be useful, such as ordering deadlines, special offers or discounts, satisfaction guarantees, etc. If you're planning to purchase more than one species, create a separate comparison chart for each type of animal. If a farm you're considering offers two or more of the species you're looking for, list it on each comparison chart. (The farm may be your best choice for one species, but not the others.)

Below are 14 common criteria you may want to consider, but there could be many others that are of personal importance to you. To avoid becoming overwhelmed, try to limit your selection process to just the three or four factors that are of greatest relevance for you and your household. One or more of the first three criteria listed below are often deal-breakers for people, and if this is the case for you, use these as initial "screeners" to weed out farms that definitely won't meet your needs. A farm must pass this screening before even being added to the list for consideration.

Share Size Options

First and foremost, the farm must offer the type of meat you're looking for in the share size you want (as determined in Chapter 3). If you're looking for a whole or half animal, this is rarely a problem. Quarter beefs are also relatively common. Eighths and sixteenths of beef, as well as quarter (or smaller) shares of hogs or lambs are more difficult to come by, however.

Availability

Unlike in a grocery store, meat purchased in bulk isn't necessarily available year-round. Farmers generally have specific times of year that they prefer to harvest, and some animals, such as lambs, are highly seasonal. If you don't want to wait several months for your meat, you'll need to limit your search to those farmers who will have meat ready sooner rather than later. When inquiring about availability, be sure to ask when the animals will be slaughtered *and* when processing by the butcher will be completed. For some meats, there can be a considerable gap between the two (dry aging beef and smoking or curing pork can add weeks at the butcher).

Distance

For the safety of your meat and for your own convenience, you don't want to spend hours in the car picking up your purchase and bringing it home. Limit your search to a one-hour driving radius from your home, or less based on your preferences. It's important to note that in most cases you'll be picking up the meat from the butcher, not from the farmer, so the butcher's address is usually the important one. (Farmers are usually located near the butchers they use, but a distance of 15–20 miles isn't uncommon, and, depending on your location, that difference can work in or against your favor.) Some producers may offer on-farm pickup, and others may be able to bring your order to a local farmers market. A small minority of farmers offer home delivery (occasionally free, but usually for an additional charge).

Price

For most individuals, price is a top consideration when selecting a farmer. As discussed in Chapter 3, meat sold this way is almost always charged at a per-pound price based on hanging weight. Doing a price comparison between farmers, however, can be complicated by the fact that some roll the butcher's processing fees into the per-pound price they quote customers, while others do not. Be sure you're comparing apples to apples (i.e., total per-pound price, including all processing charges) when price shopping. If a farm's website indicates that the processing fees will be paid separately and only includes a vague statement such as "plus butcher's fees" or "plus cut and wrap," you will need to contact the farm's contracted butcher to find out exactly what these fees will be. Even if a website includes very exact information about the cost for processing the meat, it's still a good idea to call the butcher to confirm these numbers—websites are not always up-to-date and the butcher may have changed their fees without telling the farmer.

If total purchase price, not just the per-pound rate, is also important to you, you will need to estimate this for each prospective farmer by multiplying the per-pound rate by the estimated hanging weight. Because hanging weight estimates are just that—estimates—this type of comparison is really only useful when comparing farmers who raise different breeds that vary substantially in size from each other or who harvest significantly earlier or later in an animal's lifetime than the average (thus yielding a smaller or larger hanging weight).

Organic

For a farmer to advertise their meat as organic, their farm must be certified, either by the federal government (to carry the "USDA Organic" label) or by a state agency. Many small farmers choose not to go through the state or federal certification process because of the cost involved. However, many farmers point out that they use organic feeds and follow organic farming practices, such as abstaining from the use of pesticides. These farmers may meet most or even all of the requirements needed to carry an organic label, but in the absence of an official certification, it becomes your responsibility to determine just how closely they're adhering to the "spirit of the law." If buying organic is a top consideration, you will either need to find a farmer with organic certification or do your due diligence to satisfy yourself that their claims about organic feed and practices are true.

Animal Feed

Any farm you're considering should guarantee that its meat is free of hormones and antibiotics. Cattle and lambs should be 100% grass-fed and grass-finished. Feed for hogs and chickens, however, can vary significantly, so if you're looking for these meats and believe strongly in the health benefits or risks of certain feed ingredients or characteristics, you may want to make this one of your search criteria. Do you want to purchase meat only from animals fed organic feed? Non-GMO feed? Soy- and/ or corn-free feed? Feed produced on-farm or sourced locally? Are hogs given whey or finished on apples, hazelnuts, or something else that will give their meat a special flavor?

Animal Welfare

For most people buying meat this way, the humane treatment of the animals is a top concern. While all small-scale farmers will claim that their animals are raised naturally and humanely, this is a broad and ambiguous claim. Thus, it's up to you to decide what qualifies as "natural and humane" and whether or not a specific farm lives up to your definition.

There are several national animal welfare certification programs, the most well respected of which are the Animal Welfare Approved certification program conducted by A Greener World, Global Animal Partnership's 5-Step Animal Welfare Program (used for all meats carried by Whole Foods), and the Certified Humane label used by the Humane Farm Animal Care group (see the Resources section for links). Unfortunately, as with organic certification, few small-scale farmers—even those that meet or exceed the standards for animal welfare certification—carry these labels because the certification process is often costly. You may, however, want to use these organizations' guidelines as a metric against which to judge the farms you're considering.

In addition to factors that should be considered mandatory (such as continuous pasture access, no grain for steers and lambs, and no use of hormones and antibiotics), some of the most common welfare concerns include the use of branding, how often animals are moved to fresh pasture, how long young animals are allowed to stay with their mothers, and where and how they are slaughtered (see below). If there are specific aspects of the animals' car and living conditions that concern you, be sure to ask the farmer directly about these. As will be discussed toward the end of this chapter, an in-person visit to the farm is the best way to satisfy any welfare-related concerns you may have.

Breeds Raised

Some customers are looking to purchase meat that comes from a particular breed. Usually this is because of taste preferences, since the flavor, texture, and leanness of meat can vary significantly from one breed to another. Some may wish to seek out particular heritage breeds. Heritage breeds are traditional livestock breeds that were raised before the rise of industrialized agriculture. These breeds tend to be hardy and are well-suited to pasture-based farming. In many cases, these heritage breeds are threatened or endangered and now raised only on small-scale family farms. By purchasing meat from heritage breed animals, customers support the farms that raise them and thus help to perpetuate the breed as a whole and the history and traditional foodways it represents. Appendix A lists the breeds most commonly raised on small-scale farms.

Diversified Farm

A diversified farm is one that raises a variety of animals and plants. They are in stark contrast to the large monoculture farms that now dominate American industrialized agriculture. Diversified farms follow biodynamic farming practices (for example, using waste from farm animals as fertilizer) and are generally considered to be more sustainable and better for the environment than single-use farms. And, depending on what you're looking for, they may be a "one-stop shopping" solution, thereby simplifying the purchase process.

Slaughter and Processing Location

In some cases, animals are killed on the farm, while in others they are trucked to an off-site facility (either a local butcher or a separate abattoir). Farmers who practice on-farm slaughter argue that it causes less stress for the animal, since it is not being confined and moved to an unfamiliar location. It is important to note, however, that meat from animals slaughtered on-farm cannot be sold at retail and is only available for personal consumption by the animal's owner, the owner's family, and the owner's nonpaying guests. Thus, even though it seems as if you're purchasing meat when you buy a quarter beef or a half hog, you're actually purchasing partial ownership of that animal and can thus receive the meat as a "dividend" of that ownership.

Animals slaughtered and processed off the farm can be handled at either a custom exempt meat processor or in a federally or state-inspected facility. Custom exempt facilities are still expected to meet strict sanitation requirements and are regularly monitored by state inspectors, but they are not under continuous inspection. As with on-farm slaughter, this meat cannot be sold at retail and is only intended for the owner's consumption. On the other hand, meat from animals slaughtered and processed at a federally or state-inspected facility can be sold at farmers markets, grocery stores, restaurants, and other retail outlets because it has met the highest legal standards for safety.

Cut Customization

In most cases, the butcher will allow you to make basic decisions about how your order is processed (for example, whether steaks are bone-in or boneless or how many pork chops to a package). The most common butchering choices you'll be asked to make for each species are covered in Appendix A. In general, the larger a percentage of an animal you buy, the greater freedom you have to customize your order, since you're sharing that individual animal with fewer people. Beyond these basic cut instructions, certain operations are much more willing than others to process an animal to a customer's exact specifications. If you want to ensure you'll have total control over how your order is processed and packaged, or if you know you'll want a number of specialty cuts, it's important to speak to the butcher that will be used ahead of time to make sure that they're willing and able to accommodate you.

On the other hand, in some situations a farmer and butcher may agree to only offer a "standard cut" to customers buying in bulk in order to keep processing time and effort (and thus costs) down. The butcher's "standard cut" represents the simplest and most commonly requested breakdown of cuts and allows for little if any customization by the customer. A standard cut will be perfectly fine for the majority of customers but can frustrate those who want more control.

Type of Packaging

Your processed order will be packaged in one of two ways: it will either be vacuum-sealed in one or two layers of plastic or it will be wrapped (usually double-wrapped) in white freezer paper. Freezer paper is similar to regular butcher paper but has a plastic coating on one side to help keep moisture in and air out. Vacuum sealing costs more and is less likely to be used by small butcher operations because the machines can be quite expensive. Meat wrapped properly in freezer paper will last at least a year, but over longer time periods vacuum-sealed packages enjoy a slight advantage in preventing freezer burn. When defrosting meat, there's a greater chance that packages wrapped in freezer paper will leak compared to those vacuum-sealed in plastic, although both options are usually quite secure. In almost all cases, a butcher will use one or the other method, not both. So if the packaging is important to you, be sure to ask about it ahead of time.

Reviews

As with any other important purchase, it's a good idea to look for reviews of the farms (and their contracted butchers) you're choosing between. You may be able to find reviews on Google, Yelp, or the farm/butcher's own website or Facebook page, and you may be able to solicit opinions on sites like Nextdoor and community-specific forums on sites like Reddit. It's important to remember, however, that small, highly local operations such as these rarely have a large collection of online reviews, so a lack of these shouldn't surprise or worry you. And, because individuals are most apt to leave a review only if their experience was inordinately good or bad or if they personally know the farmer or butcher, the reviews you do find may not be truly representative of the full range of customers' experiences.

Option to Sample

Some farms provide the chance to "try before you buy" (or, more accurately, "buy a little before you buy a lot"). This is a much better way than reading reviews to ensure that you'll be happy with your bulk purchase. Some farms sell at local farmers markets or offer retail sales at an on-site farm store. Larger producers may even sell their meat to local high-end grocery stores or meat markets. Farmers who use custom exempt butchers and thus cannot sell their meat at retail may still be willing to give you a small sample for free.

If possible, it's best to try both a "low-end" cut (such as chuck roast or ground pork) and a "high end" cut (such as a ribeye steak or pork chop) when sampling. This will give you a better idea of the spectrum of flavor, texture, and tenderness you can expect. Prepare samples using simple, familiar recipes that will make it easy for you to evaluate the meat. If comparing similar samples from multiple farms, be sure to cook them all the same way to keep your judgements as fair as possible. While some farmers also sell their meat to local restaurants, this is not the best setting to sample their product, since your experience will be heavily influenced by the restaurant's particular preparation.

Conducting a Farm Visit

If, after doing your research, you still have questions or lingering concerns about a farm—or if you simply want to get a better "feel" for the farmer and where and how the animals are raised—you may wish to make a farm visit. Some farms have regular visiting hours, but most farmers arrange visits only by appointment because of their busy work schedule. All farmers should be amenable to a farm visit. If a producer you're considering refuses to let you visit the farm or seems particularly evasive about nailing down a day and time, this is a major red flag and that farm should be immediately removed from your consideration list.

Farm visits allow you to see for yourself how the animals are raised. This can be especially helpful in light of the fact that most small-scale farms do not operate with organic or animal welfare certifications. Seeing the animals' environment and how the farmer interacts with them will help you to better judge whether the farm lives up to the claims it makes and to your own quality standards. It's also a great way to build a more personal connection with the farmer. If you have specific questions you'd like answered, be sure to write them down ahead of time.

What About Finding Your Own Butcher?

Some farmers will require you to make your own arrangements for the slaughter and processing of an animal you buy from them. While this does allow you the flexibility to shop around for a butcher with particularly good prices or one willing to do the custom cuts you're looking for, it makes the research process longer and more complicated and will require more attention and coordination from you once the animal is ready to be slaughtered. Unless you happen to already have an established relationship with a butcher, farms that require you to make your own arrangements should be automatically dropped from your list of candidates. In the future, once you've had more experience with the process of buying meat in bulk, you may want to consider such farms, but they aren't a good option for those just starting out.

Once you've filled out your comparison chart(s) based on your own unique priorities, the "winner" for each type of animal you're searching for should become clear. If you can't decide between two or more prospective farms, you can either select one at random or find additional criteria to use as a "tie breaker."

In the next chapter, we'll discuss how the purchasing and pick-up process works.

CHAPTER 6

PAYING FOR AND PICKING UP YOUR MEAT

Once you've decided on what, how much, and from where you'll buy, it's time to make your purchase. Unlike buying meat at a grocery store, however, buying a quarter, half, or whole animal isn't accomplished in a single transaction. Instead, buying meat in bulk is a multi-step event that can span several weeks or even months. While this may sound daunting or cumbersome, the process is actually quite simple and straightforward. Most farmers and butchers do an excellent job of walking first-timers through the process, but it's helpful to know ahead of time what to expect.

Step 1: Putting Down a Deposit

After you've selected a farmer to buy from, you'll need to pay a deposit to secure your purchase. Because raising and harvesting animals follows a predictable pattern from year to year, farmers know (at least approximately) when each animal will be slaughtered and usually accept deposits months in advance of that date. In fact, popular local farms often sell out of available animals quickly, so place your deposit as early as possible.

Deposit amounts are usually based on the anticipated final cost of the meat, so they can vary widely based on what you're buying. A half lamb might require only a $30 or $50 deposit, while a whole beef might require a deposit of $300 or more. In most cases, deposits are nonrefundable (unless something unexpected happens to the animal before its anticipated slaughter date), so you should be absolutely certain about your purchase before putting down the deposit. Many farms accept online credit and debit payments, but in some cases you may need to mail or hand-deliver a check.

Some farmers may allow you to specify a general size preference (large or small), which they will try to accommodate when assigning animals to buyers at the time of slaughter. If you're purchasing a front or hind quarter (rather than a mixed quarter), you'll need to make your choice when you pay the deposit.

Once you've paid your deposit, there's nothing more you need to do until the animal is slaughtered. It's important to realize that although farmers have a target date set for when their animals will be harvested, the actual slaughter date may be several weeks earlier or later, depending on factors such as the farmer's and butcher's schedules, the growth rate of the animals, and weather conditions. As the time draws closer, farmers will usually provide their customers with a more accurate slaughter date.

Step 2: Paying the Balance and Providing Cut Instructions

A day or two after the animal has been slaughtered, you'll be contacted by the farmer and presented with a bill based on the actual hanging weight of your portion of the animal. (The farmer gets this weight from the butcher.) You'll pay the total amount due, minus the deposit amount paid earlier. In some cases, the farmer pays the butcher for their services and passes this cost on to you in their final bill. In other cases, the farmer's bill only reflects what you owe them—you'll pay the farmer that amount now and pay the butcher's processing fees directly to the butcher when you pick up your meat.

Once you've been notified that the animal has been slaughtered, you'll need to provide the butcher with your cut instructions. The farmer will specify whether the butcher will call you or you'll need to call them. (However, if you're expecting a call but haven't heard from anyone after a day or two, make sure to reach out to the butcher, as it's important to get your cut instructions in on time.)

Cut instructions are the specifications you give the butcher about how you want your meat processed and packaged. For some, this might sound like a very intimidating task. Butchers, however, are very good about walking customers through their choices and explaining options. They will ask you a series of questions in order to fill out their cut sheet. Some questions relate to packaging and should be easy to answer based on your family size and cooking habits. For example, you will probably be asked to specify whether you want two or four pork chops per package, or whether you want your ground beef in one- or two-pound increments. Other questions will relate to how the meat will be cut and processed. How thick do you want your steaks? What sausage flavors do you want? Do you want a rack of lamb or multiple rib chops? If you're unsure what to pick or unclear about how your choices might affect other aspects of your order, the butcher will be happy to answer your questions and offer suggestions.

Before speaking with the butcher, it's a good idea to review the most common cutting and packaging options for the animal you've purchased, listed in Appendix A. Write down any questions that come to mind so you'll have them ready when you're on the phone. You may also want to make a note of any regional or specialty cuts you like (for example, steak tips or a tri-tip roast) so you'll remember to mention them; these cuts may not be standard, but the butcher can usually provide them if you ask.

On the other end of the spectrum, for those who are excited about giving the butcher a very detailed list of highly customized cuts, it's important to realize that the butcher may not be able to accommodate all these special requests. (As discussed in the previous chapter, if a high level of customization is something you're looking for, you'll need to take this into consideration when selecting a farmer.)

Once the butcher has your cut instructions, they can begin processing your meat. The time needed for this depends on both the species and the workload of the butcher. Lamb and chicken do not need to be aged and are usually ready a week or so after slaughter unless the butcher is particularly busy. Beef should be aged at least two weeks before being cut and packaged, as this allows enzymes present in the meat time to begin breaking down muscle fibers, which improves the meat's texture and flavor. Because of this added aging time, beef is usually ready three to four weeks after slaughter. For pork, fresh cuts such as pork chops and ribs can be processed in the week or so following slaughter. Smoked or cured cuts such as bacon, ham, and hocks, however, require extra attention and time—usually an additional one to two weeks. If you've ordered a whole or half hog, you may be able to pick up your purchase in two separate trips, or you may choose or be asked to wait until everything is ready.

Step 3: Getting Your Meat Home

While a few farms may offer the option of home delivery, in most cases you'll need to pick up your meat yourself—usually from the butcher who processed it. In some instances, however, you may be able to pick up your purchase at a local farmers market or at the farm itself.

The butcher will call you when your order is ready to be picked up. You may also receive a call or email from the farmer when your order is available. Generally, you can stop by any time the butcher is open, but to expedite the pick-up process you may want to call ahead to let them know you're coming. Working farms are very busy places, so if you're picking up from the farmer directly you'll need to work with them to arrange a pick-up day and time. Most butchers are happy to hold your meat for a week or so, but if you won't be able to retrieve it for a while (if, for example, you're out of town), be sure to discuss this with the butcher. If you think your order should be ready but you haven't heard from the butcher or the farmer, it never hurts to make a quick inquiry by phone.

Before you head out to collect your meat, make sure your freezer has been running for at least 24 hours and whatever organization system you plan to use is in place (see "Organizing Your Freezer" in Chapter 7). Call the butcher (or farmer) to find out if and how the meat will be boxed. Some butchers may pack the meat in insulated Styrofoam coolers, but most will use cardboard boxes or large heavy-duty trash bags. Some may require you to bring your own containers. If this is the case, large plastic coolers are best, but milk crates, large Rubbermaid bins, cardboard boxes, or heavy-duty plastic or canvas bags will all work. Bring more containers than you think you'll need and make sure you have plenty of space available in your vehicle.

If butchering fees are due at pick-up, check which forms of payment are accepted—some smaller operations may not take credit cards. If your order included bones, organ meats, or other offal, check to make sure that these have been included when you pick up your purchase. Because these are less commonly asked for items, they may be accidentally overlooked when employees are getting your order ready.

Although your meat will stay solidly frozen for at least a couple hours outside of a freezer, aim to pick up your purchase either in the morning or evening if possible to avoid higher temperatures at midday. Bring several large towels or a reflective sunshade to cover the filled containers to help keep the meat insulated. Depending on the ambient temperature, you may also want to run the air conditioning. Once you've picked up your purchase, head straight home; any other errands (including getting gas) should be done before arriving at the butcher.

If the butcher did not provide you with an itemized list of cuts and weights, it's best to catalogue this information on your freezer inventory now before moving the meat into your freezer (see "Creating and Maintaining a Freezer Inventory" in Chapter 7). If you're pressed for time, you can save this step for later, but aim to do it as soon as possible. Find a large flat surface (the floor is fine) and group packages together based on cut. Once all the meat has been sorted, begin filling out your freezer inventory, noting how many packages of each cut you have. Use a food scale to weigh each package and record the information on your inventory. In most cases, all the packages of a particular cut will be very close to one another in weight, so, unless a particular package looks significantly larger or smaller than its kin, you only need to weigh one package from each group.

After sitting out during transit and the inventorying process, your packages of meat are likely to have acquired a coating of condensation. To help keep your freezer as frost-free as possible, use a towel to dry off each package before placing it inside. This is especially helpful if you're using a chest freezer or a manual defrost upright freezer.

Making Additional Purchases

You'll follow the above steps every time you make a bulk meat purchase, whether it's from the same farmer and butcher or not. As you can see, there's often a significant amount of time between putting down a deposit and actually getting the meat into your freezer. Adequately accounting for this lag becomes very important when making subsequent purchases, whether you're restocking your supply of the same meat or adding another species to your freezer. If, for instance, you wait until your freezer is completely empty before ordering more meat, you may have to wait six months or longer for the next available animal to reach slaughter weight and be processed and packaged. On the other hand, if your next meat order is ready before you've had a chance to adequately eat down your previous orders, you won't have enough room in your freezer.

Buying from the same farmer can make timing your subsequent purchases easier, since the size of the animals they raise, when they slaughter, and how far in advance they begin accepting deposits are all likely to remain consistent from year to year. Unfortunately, this isn't always an option: you may want to add another species that that farmer doesn't raise, or you may need to restock at a time of year when that farmer isn't harvesting any animals.

To determine the best time to begin your next purchase, you'll need to first determine when you'll have enough freezer space available. To do this, you must know four things:

1. How many pounds of food your freezer can hold when full, either based on the general rule of thumb of 22.5 pounds per cubic foot if it's a chest freezer and 20 pounds per cubic foot if it's an upright freezer, or, preferably, on your personal experiences with past orders.

2. How many pounds of meat your freezer is currently holding.

3. Approximately how many pounds your purchase will be (based either on a farmer's estimate or the rough estimates provided in Chapter 3).

4. How much meat your household is eating per month (see the "Pacing Yourself" section in Chapter 8).

Once you have this information, figuring out when you'll have the available space becomes a simple math problem. Begin by subtracting the amount your freezer is currently holding from its maximum capacity to determine how much free space you already have. Next, subtract this free space from the anticipated size of the meat you want to purchase; this is the amount of additional space you'll need to be available. Then divide that number by the amount of meat your household consumes each month, rounding up to create a cushion, to calculate how many months it will take you to get the space you need. For example, imagine your freezer can hold approximately 200 pounds of meat but is currently only holding 135 pounds. You want to buy a quarter beef, which the farmer estimates will yield approximately 110 pounds of meat. Your family is eating about 10 pounds of meat a month. Based on this information, you'll need to free up enough currently in-use space for 45 pounds of meat (110 - [200-135]). At your family's consumption level, this will take approximately 5 months (45 ÷ 10, rounded up).

Once you have a "finally enough room in the freezer" date, you can use this to select a farmer and time your purchase. Let's imagine that, in the example above, you made these calculations in May, meaning you'll have enough space for your beef purchase in October. The farmer you initially spoke with is taking deposits now and planning to harvest his steers in early August with the processed meat available at the end of that month, but you now know that you probably won't have enough freezer space by then. Another farmer is planning to harvest his steers, which will be a comparable size, in November and will begin taking deposits in July. You can set a reminder for yourself to put down a deposit in July, assured that by November you'll definitely have the freezer space you'll need.

———————

Now that you've done the work of finding, purchasing, and bringing home your bulk meat order, you're probably more than ready to start enjoying it. But first, you'll want to make sure it's well organized and inventoried and that you're creating a weekly meal plan. These steps will be discussed in the final two chapters and will make using your meat hassle-free on a day-to-day basis.

CHAPTER 7

FREEZER ORGANIZATION AND THE FREEZER INVENTORY

Having a freezer full of locally raised, grass-fed meat is undeniably satisfying, but that large stockpile can quickly turn from bounty to burden if you don't stay organized. Luckily, there are only two elements needed to achieve this: a system for keeping your meat physically organized within your freezer and a freezer inventory that allows you to see, at a glance, what you have on hand.

Organizing Your Freezer

The first step to making good use of the meat you've purchased is being able to actually locate what you're looking for. If finding a particular item always requires a frustrating 20-minute rummage through the freezer that leaves you with numb hands and a sore back from being bent over so long, you'll soon find yourself avoiding the freezer—and its contents—altogether. Having a well-organized freezer allows you to quickly and easily find what you're looking for. Organization is especially important when using chest freezers because they lack the convenient shelves of upright models.

Grouping Packages and Using Containers

To make specific packages easier to find, they should be kept together with other similar items. How you divvy up your meat is completely up to you, but the most commonly used distinctions are by species (beef with beef, pork with pork, etc.) and/or by general type of cut (steaks and chops, ground beef and sausage, roasts and stew meat, organs meats, etc.). Whether you choose to use one system or the other—or both—will depend on what makes most sense for you given the meat you have and the size of your freezer. For example, if you only have beef in your freezer, of course it makes sense to separate packages by cut. Someone who has a small freezer might decide to group their beef steaks and pork chops together, since they're a similar type of cut (suitable for quick, high-heat cooking) and combine their packages of ground beef and sausage together as well. Another person with a larger freezer might decide to separate packages by both animal and cut type, with beef steaks, ground beef, pork chops, and sausage all kept separately. Keep in mind that the more similarly shaped items are, the easier it is to efficiently pack them together.

Once you've decided how you're going to separate your meat, you need to find a way to actually keep it separate. If you're using an upright freezer, this may be as simple as stacking packages together on designated shelves. If you're using a chest freezer, however, you'll need to find some form of container. These can take many forms—milk crates, large plastic storage bins, cardboard file boxes, heavy-duty canvas bags, etc. The only requirements for a container are that it be sturdy enough to be lifted in and out of the freezer when full, won't be damaged by the cold temperature, and can be stacked with relative ease.

The key is finding containers that fit the dimensions of your freezer well. The containers themselves take up space (especially if they have thick plastic sides), and the empty space between containers must either be filled with loose packages or given up. To maximize usable freezer space, find containers that fit the freezer's internal dimensions as snugly as possible while still allowing for enough space for you to get your hands around them to lift them up. Unfortunately, since a freezer's dimensions are model-specific, there's no shortcut to finding containers that are a perfect fit—you'll have to take measurements, shop around, and crunch the numbers. Use a tape measure to determine each internal dimension of your freezer: top to bottom, side to side, and back to front. If you have a chest freezer with one or more hanging baskets, be sure to measure both from the bottom of the freezer to the top of the freezer and from the bottom of the freezer to the bottom of the basket. If your chest freezer has a "shelf" on one side (under which the motor is housed), be sure to measure its dimensions as well. Remember to allow for enough space to get your hands around each container and to slide a basket (if you have one) over a container.

When looking for containers that best fit your freezer's dimensions, it's important to keep container size and weight when full in mind. If, for example, the internal dimensions of your freezer are 38" long x 26" deep x 35" high, you could fill that space with three 36" x 24" x 10" plastic bins stacked on top of each other. But such large containers will be unwieldy and very heavy when filled with packages of meat. In this case, it would be much better to get a larger number of smaller containers—for instance, perhaps six 18" x 12" x 10" containers. Remember, however, that unless your containers fit together perfectly like pieces of a puzzle, the more small containers you use, the more freezer space you'll lose.

While places like The Container Store have numerous higher-end options for containers, be sure to check retailers like Target, Lowe's, and Staples for potentially less expensive possibilities, as well as taking a look around Craigslist, local yard sales, and your own garage or basement. If you're having trouble finding rigid boxes or bins that meet your size needs, consider heavy-duty canvas or vinyl bags, which can easily conform to the space they're placed in.

If you're using many containers, you may want to label each to help quickly identify the contents. When placing containers in the freezer, place the ones you'll be accessing most frequently toward the top if using a chest freezer or toward the front at eye level if using an upright freezer.

An Alternative Option

While grouping packages together based on type of animal and/or broad categories of cut is the most common—and usually most useful—method for organizing a freezer, there's another option that may appeal to you.

The "Bag Method" is a time-based organizational system. In this method, you calculate how many pounds of meat you and your family will eat in a given time period (typically a week, but perhaps two) and find a combination of packages that equals or comes close to that weight and place these together in a plastic grocery bag that is then tied close. For example, if you know your family typically eats 4.5 pounds of meat per week, you might include a 3-pound ham and a 1.5-pound package of stew meat in one bag, two 1-pound packages of ground lamb and a 2.5-pound chuck roast in a second bag, and a single whole chicken in a third. Then, at the beginning of each time period, you select a bag at random to move to your refrigerator (or fridge freezer if each bag covers a longer time period) and create a meal plan around whatever's inside.

This method is great for people who don't mind being surprised, and it's particularly helpful if you need to maximize the square footage of your freezer, since bags can be layered on top of one another so that all available freezer space is used. It can also make meal planning for the week a bit easier, since you can focus on choosing recipes to suit whatever cuts of meat the bag contained. But apportioning all the meat this way takes more effort upfront, and you're at the mercy of the contents of whichever bag you choose. While you could certainly put back a bag if you didn't feel like having whatever it contained that particular week and choose another, this system is not effective if you or other family members frequently crave specific foods. If you absolutely *must* satisfy your yen for lamb chops with mint sauce and your four-year-old is going through a phase where he only wants to eat burgers, you're not going to be able to quickly locate the specific items you need with this system. This system can also make it more difficult to meet meal needs for specific occasions. For example, if you plan to make a ham on Easter, you'll need to sort through your freezer to find a bag that contains a ham.

Creating and Maintaining a Freezer Inventory

Sorting the items in your freezer to make finding packages easier is only the first half of an effective organizational plan. The second is creating and maintaining a freezer inventory. A freezer inventory is a list of your freezer's contents that allows you to quickly see what you have without needing to actually open the freezer.

Inventory Options

You have several options when it comes to creating a freezer inventory, so choose the one that works best for your situation. The first is creating a paper inventory. This can be as simple as using the invoice your butcher gave you, or you may choose to hand-write or type out a list. This sheet can be taped to or near the freezer for convenience and items can be crossed off as they're removed and used. For cases in which you have a number of packages of the same item, you can use tick marks to keep track of how many you've used and then cross the item off completely once all packages have been eaten.

You can also keep your inventory on a small dry erase board or chalkboard. The ability to both easily erase and add items will help keep your inventory neater and easier to read and makes this an excellent choice if you anticipate frequently adding items to your freezer (additional meat purchases, large batches of things like stock or pasta sauce, etc.).

The third option is to keep an electronic inventory—on your computer, your phone, or saved on the cloud through a service like Google Drive so that it can be accessed from multiple devices. An electronic inventory is easy to add to, subtract from, and rearrange. If you save the inventory on your phone or in the cloud, you can access it when away from home, making grocery shopping a bit easier if you haven't had time to meal plan. This format is also best if you're planning to keep a lot of optional information on your inventory (see below). However, because an electronic inventory isn't always in plain view, you may have trouble remembering to update it when you add or remove something. And if multiple people will be getting in and out of the freezer, you'll need to make sure that each person has access to and the ability to edit the electronic inventory.

What to Include in Your Freezer Inventory

Regardless of the medium used, a freezer inventory should include the following, set up as column headings:

- Cut of meat/contents of package ("Italian sausage," "whole chicken," "sirloin steak," etc.). If it's important to you, include the number of individual items in each package ("Italian sausage (4 links)" or "sirloin steak (2x)"). Be sure to arrange your inventory so that the list follows a logical order. For instance, in addition to grouping beef items together, list the different types of steaks one after another before moving on to the different types of roasts.

- Weight of each package. It's fine to round to the nearest quarter- or half-pound. In most cases all packages of the same item will be very close in weight, but if not, you can either list exactly how many packages are each weight (for example, "1.5lbs (2x), 2.5lbs (1x)") or you can simply give a range ("1.5–2.5lbs"). If the butcher's inventory or the package labels do not include weights, you'll need to use a food scale to weigh each package.

- Total Packages. Knowing how many packages of each cut you started with is helpful for determining how quickly you're eating a particular item and may be useful to refer back to when making future bulk meat purchases.

- Packages Used/Packages Remaining. If you'll be using tick marks on a paper inventory, you'll want to keep track of packages used. If using an erasable or electronic inventory, you can keep track of either or both.

- Packages/Pounds Eaten This Month. To ensure that your meat lasts as long as you need it to last, it's important to set a limit of a certain number of pounds or packages of meat per month (for more information, see the next chapter). The Pounds/Packages Eaten This Month column allows you to track your monthly consumption and can be cleared at the beginning of each month. So, in addition to noting when you use an item in the permanent Packages Used and/or Packages Remaining column(s), you'll also put that information in the revolving monthly column. (If tracking pounds per month, multiply number of packages removed by the weight of each package.)

In addition to the above, you may also want to include some or all of the following, depending on how much space you have on your inventory and what details are important to you:

- Date Added. Because most or all of the contents of your freezer will be meat purchased in bulk at one time, it's not necessary to list the date added for each package. You may, however, want to note the date that all the meat from a particular purchase was placed in the freezer (for example, the quarter beef was added May 15, 2018). Because meat purchased this way is very fresh and well-wrapped, keeping track of the date added is less about making sure you use packages before they go bad and more about keeping track of how quickly you're eating down your freezer. If, however, you have a lot of items coming in and out of the freezer, you may want to include a package's add date on the inventory.

- Date Last Used. If using an erasable or electronic inventory, you may want to note the date you remove an item, updating that date the next time you remove another package of the same item. This can be useful if you're trying to more evenly stagger your consumption of particular items. For example, if you see from your inventory that you had one of your two packages of filet mignon two weeks ago, you'll probably want to wait a few months before having that second package. Or perhaps after looking at your inventory you'll see that you haven't had one of your whole chickens in a while.

- Time to Defrost. This is information that will be filled in as you use your meat and, once you know it, can be helpful for future meal planning. The first time you take out a particular item, write down how long it takes to defrost in the refrigerator or in a sink full of cold water.

- Notes. This is a catch-all for any other information you may want to keep track of, and the notes section is generally something that's filled out as you go through the meat in your freezer so that it can be referred back to later. To improve your experience buying bulk meat in the future, you may want to note if there are any changes to the cut instructions you would make next time (larger/smaller packages, grinding certain tougher cuts, sausage flavors you particularly liked or didn't like, etc.). You can also leave yourself reminders for cooking instructions or favorite recipes. But because including a notes section on an inventory can clutter it up very quickly, it's usually best to keep these notes in a separate document.

Tips for Maintaining a Freezer Inventory

A freezer inventory is only beneficial if it's accurate and faithfully kept up-to-date. If you find yourself forgetting to update your inventory when you add or remove items (which is especially likely if your inventory is not physically attached to or near the freezer), consider putting a reminder someplace you're likely to see it, such as taped to the inside of the freezer door or in a highlighted, all-caps note at the top of the document you use for meal planning. It's also a good idea to re-inventory the contents of the freezer every four to six months to double-check that your records are accurate.

If you're at the point where you've made a subsequent purchase of the same type of meat and now have both new and old packages of the same cuts, it's best to list these separately on your freezer inventory—for example: "top sirloin (2017)" and "top sirloin (2018)." This way, it's easy to keep track of which items from the older order still need to be consumed before you begin enjoying the same cuts from the new order. (Older packages should also be kept on top or in front of newer ones so that they're more accessible.)

Because knowing how many total packages you began with can be a useful planning tool for making future bulk purchases, do not completely erase or delete an item when all packages have been removed. If using paper, dry erase board, or chalkboard, you can simply cross out the item (ensuring that the words underneath are still legible) or place an X in front of the item name. If using an electronic inventory, you can use the strikethrough tool or move the item to a separate part of the document.

Appendix C includes a sample freezer inventory and a blank template that you can customize and either print or copy for your own use.

———

Keeping your freezer's contents organized and being able to quickly know exactly what you have without digging around go a long way to ensuring you'll actually use the meat you've purchased. There are, however, other important strategies you'll need to use in order to make dining from your freezer a regular, hassle-free habit. In the final chapter, we'll explore the more "hands on" side of the equation, including meal planning and cooking techniques.

CHAPTER 8

MEAL PLANNING, PACING, AND PREPARATION

Even though you may have over a hundred pounds of high-quality meat close at hand, it still takes a bit of forethought and skill to turn it into delicious dishes. Regular meal planning is an essential component of bulk buying that cannot be skipped. You will likely also want to monitor and control the speed at which your inventory of each species is eaten. And, depending on what you've purchased, you may need to make small adjustments to your preparation and cooking methods. But, with these habits and techniques in place, "eating down the freezer" will quickly become faster and easier than shopping for dinner at the meat counter of your grocery store.

Meal Planning

Whether or not they actually do it, by now most people are aware that meal planning is an excellent way to reduce food spending and waste, streamline grocery shopping, and avoid unhealthy impulse meals. While planning out meals in advance can benefit anyone, it's a necessity for individuals or families who've bought meat in bulk. The very fact that meat from the freezer will need at least a day or two to defrost in the fridge means that you'll need to be thinking ahead a few days. And without a plan in place, a freezer full of meat can quickly begin to feel overwhelming.

Meal planning with your freezer meat may be mandatory, but that doesn't mean it needs to be complicated or time-consuming. While there are plenty of resources that provide in-depth guidance on meal planning in general, you may find the tips below particularly useful. If you've decided to use the "Bag Method" described in the previous chapter, meal planning will be slightly simplified—you will simply remove a bag and construct a meal plan around the contents of that bag.

Do It Weekly and Make It Overlapping

While some hardcore planners swear by a monthly meal plan, for most people a weekly meal plan is the most manageable. While your current hankerings and intriguing new recipes may be floating around in your mind throughout the week, choose one day each week to actually sit down and write out a concrete meal plan. While many people use Sunday as their planning day, you can use whichever day works best for you. And, since meals—especially those that involve thawing frozen meat—usually require a day or more of forethought, it's important to overlap your weekly meal plans so that you aren't thinking up tonight's meal on planning day. For example, if you do your weekly meal plan on Monday, make sure it extends through the following Monday (or, better yet, through the following Tuesday) rather than ending it on Sunday night.

Take Your Calendar into Account

Before making your menu for the upcoming week, be sure to take a look at your calendar to see what events and obligations are coming up so that you can plan accordingly. Are there days when you'll be eating away from home because of celebrations or travel? Are there days when you know you'll be super busy? Don't schedule time-consuming or difficult-to-make meals on days when you have a lot of other things going on. For hectic days, quick and easy meals or leftovers are ideal. If you want to try a new recipe and aren't sure how long it will actually take to prepare, save it for a less hectic day.

Remember to Readjust

Meal plans aren't set in stone once you write them down. No matter how carefully you've laid everything out, real life often gets in the way of your meal plan. That's why it's important to do a quick reevaluation and readjustment partway through the week if new circumstances arise. The situations that are most likely to require a meal plan tweak include ending up with more/fewer leftovers than expected, unanticipated obligations outside the home that mean less time for preparing meals, and spontaneous get-togethers or meals out with friends and family. As soon as you know there'll be a disruption to your original meal plan, take a few minutes to modify your plan. This may mean adding or dropping meals, pushing certain meals back later in the week or moving them up, or choosing a quicker recipe. Thawed raw meat will last at least several days in the fridge, so you have some leeway even if you'd already begun to prep a particular recipe.

Use the One Meal Principle

If at all possible, try to limit your real meal planning to only one meal of the day (usually dinners). For breakfasts and lunches, consider cycling between a handful of easy, enjoyable options. Having to only really think about and plan for one meal each day will make the whole process faster and less stressful, especially if you're meal planning for multiple people all eating different things. (But that doesn't mean you can't use your freezer meat for some of those "standard rotation" breakfasts and lunches.) In addition, never underestimate the value of leftovers. Even if you're only concentrating your planning and cooking efforts on one meal a day, this doesn't mean you need to prepare a unique meal each day. You can make a large batch of one dish and use the leftovers for lunches or dinners later in the week or freeze them for a hassle-free option in the future.

Let the Meat be Your Guide

Most meal planning resources suggest beginning your meal plan by first taking stock of what you have already available in your refrigerator, fridge freezer, and pantry. While this is a good strategy for using up miscellaneous items before they go bad, if you have a standalone freezer full of meat, it makes the most sense to start there. Once you've selected the cut you'd like to use, you can check your fridge and cupboards for ingredients to help spark recipe ideas. If you consistently pick your fridge and pantry ingredients first and your freezer meat second, you may end up inadvertently using up one cut or type of meat much faster than the rest because it happens to work easily with the items you typically have on hand.

Make It Electronic

If your freezer inventory (discussed in the previous chapter) is kept electronically, it's best to house your meal plan in the same file (such as on a separate tab in the same Excel spreadsheet). This way, you'll be able to quickly refer back and forth between your inventory and your plan and, when you open your meal plan to see what you'll need to take out of the freezer, it will be easy to toggle to your freezer inventory and mark that item off. You can also use the same file to house your grocery list and a tally of any items in your fridge or pantry that you want to use up.

Use a Multi-Column Design

However you keep your meal plan—in an electronic file, on a whiteboard, scribbled on a scrap of paper—the setup should be the same. Write the days of the week down the left-hand side and create columns for "Breakfast," "Lunch," "Dinner," and "Prep" (you may also want to include a "Snack" column). The first three are self-explanatory, but it's the last column, "Prep," that is the secret to meal planning using your freezer meat. In this column, you'll write any prep work you'll need to do on that day for a meal in the future. Usually this means a note to move a package from the freezer to the fridge to start defrosting (allow one to three days for thawing, depending on the size of the package). It might also include reminders to go grocery shopping, begin a marinade, prepare a make-ahead dish for an event the next day, make and freeze a large batch of stock or sauce, etc.—basically, anything you need to remember to do that isn't directly connected to a meal that day. After filling in your meal plan for the week, go back and write in any relevant prep work. For example, if you plan to make a crockpot beef stew on Friday, you might make a note in Wednesday's "Prep" column to begin defrosting a package of stew meat and a note in Thursday's "Prep" column to make a batch of beef broth, some of which you'll use for the stew the next day and the rest of which you'll freeze. By figuring out the necessary prep work for each recipe when you do the meal plan, you won't have to do any thinking ahead on a day to day basis and won't find yourself unprepared when you head to the kitchen to make a recipe.

Recipes, Old and New

Making a new, delicious-looking recipe can be exciting, but preparing one or more unfamiliar dishes every week can get overwhelming. You don't have to make an ultra-creative meal plan each time. One option for adding a bit of variety and novelty without having to start from scratch is to look (in cookbooks or online) for variations on staple dishes that you and your family already like that use non-traditional ingredients that sound appealing. There are a million ways to get creative with things like meatloaf, soups and stews, meatballs, pot roast, and marinades. For example, you could cast a wide net by simply Googling "creative recipes for meatballs," or you could include keywords for specific cuisines ("Moroccan meatball recipes") or ingredients you have on hand and want to use up ("meatballs with goat cheese recipe").

Simplify Grocery Shopping

Create a grocery list as you select each meal, rather than waiting until you've finished writing up your entire meal plan. Seeing a list of ingredients you already need to buy will help you select additional recipes that use those same ingredients. This will make your trip to the store faster and cheaper and will help prevent food waste. For example, if you've already settled on making lamb chops with a Dijon-sage pan sauce, you might decide to use up the rest of the fresh sage you'll need to buy on a homemade bacon, sage, and pear pizza (rather than some other meal involving bacon from your freezer).

Take Everything Out at Once

After you've made your meal plan, take all the meat you'll need out of your standalone freezer at once and move it either to your refrigerator (if using in the next couple days) or your fridge's freezer (to move into the refrigerator a few days before it's needed). This will minimize the time you spend digging around in your standalone freezer, and the less time the freezer is open, the less electricity is needed to keep its contents at the proper temperature. Taking everything out at once also means you'll only have to update your freezer inventory once, so it's much less likely that you'll forget to mark what you've removed. If your plans change, however, and you end up not defrosting and cooking a package you placed in your refrigerator freezer, you'll need to either return it to the standalone freezer (and update the freezer inventory) or be sure to include it in the next week's meal plan.

See Appendix C for a template you can use for your weekly meal plan.

Pacing Yourself

Meal plans are an excellent way to keep track of which items you'll be using from your freezer on a weekly basis, but it's also good to keep the big picture in mind. You want to make sure the meat you've purchased lasts as long as you expect it to, and that your consumption is balanced across the different types of meat you have.

Luckily, with a few initial calculations, pacing your consumption is quite easy. First, begin by figuring out approximately how much meat of each species your family can eat each month. To do this, you can tally up either the number of packages or the combined weight of those packages for each species and divide by the number of months you want that meat to last (usually 12). Since you'll almost certainly get a result with a decimal, round down to create a little wiggle room. Going off of the number of packages makes for a faster calculation, but going off of total weight allows you to better balance your meat eating because package weights can vary enormously based on cut. When calculating, remember to include organ meats but exclude bones, skin, fat, and anything else that cannot be directly turned into a meal.

The result—whether a number of packages or a weight—represents the target you should be striving for each month. Include these targets somewhere on your freezer inventory so that you can easily refer back to them. Then, use the Packages/Pounds

Eaten This Month column (discussed in the previous chapter) to monitor your actual consumption compared to the target, adjusting your meal plans as necessary. Some months you may go slightly over, some months slightly under, but having a guideline for each species should keep you on track. (If you find that you are consistently eating well below a target, you should assume that this meat will last you longer than expected. Decide on a more realistic timeframe—perhaps 16 or 18 months—and recalculate.)

When pacing your consumption on a month-to-month basis, it's important to think about general categories of cuts in addition to total amount per species. Left to their own devices, most people will naturally gravitate toward the cuts they like most or are most familiar with preparing. They'll go through these relatively quickly and then get discouraged when they realize they have nothing but the "boring" or "weird" stuff left. You don't want to end up in month 12 with nothing in your freezer except ten packages of ground beef and the pork liver you've been too nervous about to try.

To prevent this from happening, pay attention to how often you eat certain types of cuts. To do this, you must group your meat into broad categories (either on your freezer inventory or, as discussed in the previous chapter, physically in your freezer). Below is a four-part breakdown for beef, pork, and lamb that works well.

- Prime cuts (including steaks and chops, and many people would put bacon and pork belly in this category as well): usually about 25%–30% of total non-organ meat from an animal

- Roasts (including pork shoulder, chuck roast, leg of lamb, and racks of ribs): usually about 30%–35% of non-organ meat from an animal

- Ground and stew meat (including hamburger, sausage, kebab meat, stir fry meat, etc.): usually 35%–45% of non-organ meat from an animal

- Offal (organ meats, skin, fat, and bones): varies significantly based on species and butcher

For each species you've purchased, determine what proportion of the meat falls into each category. If you don't feel like crunching the numbers, you can use the general percentages provided above. On a month-to-month basis, the ratio of the types of cuts you eat should reflect the overall ratio of cuts for each species. In most cases, this will mean eating relatively equal amounts of prime cuts and roasts and slightly more ground and stew meat. Don't worry about trying to achieve a "perfect" mix each month; the goal is simply to ensure variety throughout the entire year. Monitoring this should be as easy as looking over the Pounds/ Packages Eaten This Month column of your freezer inventory and realizing that you've already had a package of steaks and two packages of ground beef, so it's probably time for a pot roast. When it comes to the offal, challenge yourself to prepare an item from this category every two to four months, depending on what and how much you have.

Cooking Grass-Fed and Pasture-Raised Meat

The meat of pasture-raised animals is higher in protein and lower in fat than the meat of animals raised in feedlots. The leaner the meat and the older the animal it came from, the more vigilant you will need to be during preparation and cooking in order to ensure a tender, juicy result. Pastured chicken is the easiest to work with and requires few if any changes to your usual routine in the kitchen. Pastured pork also has enough fat to make cooking straightforward. The marbling of grass-fed lamb can vary significantly, and meat from very lean animals may need some additional attention. However, because lambs are harvested at a young age, their meat is extremely tender. Grass-fed beef is usually extremely lean with thick muscle fibers, meaning it will need the most care.

This doesn't mean, however, that you'll need to completely reinvent the wheel when dealing with grass-fed meat. You simply need to keep in mind the "three Ts": time, temperature, and tenderization.

Time and Temperature

During cooking, fat acts as an insulator, partially shielding the surrounding meat from the heat. Because grass-fed beef and lamb are so lean, they cook significantly faster than grain-fed beef and lamb. If you aren't monitoring the meat, it can quickly overcook and become dry and tough. Expect grass-fed beef and lamb to cook 30% faster than grain-fed, and adjust your recipes accordingly. Lean cuts of pasture-raised pork or chicken may also cook a bit faster than their grocery store counterparts.

Even without the recipe modifications that grass-fed meat sometimes requires, cooking meat for a set time is imprecise and produces highly variable results. Many factors, including altitude, ambient humidity, the thickness of your meat, and the accuracy of your oven's temperature sensor, can influence how long something needs to cook for. A much better alternative is to use an instant read probe thermometer to cook meat to the internal temperature that corresponds to the doneness level you want to achieve. The best thermometers to use can be left in the meat while it cooks and are connected by a wire to a digital display that allows you to monitor progress and set an alarm to notify you when the desired internal temperature is reached. (See the Resources section for an affordable, well-made option.) Appendix B includes internal temperature charts for beef, pork, lamb, and chicken. While you can cook your meat to whatever level of doneness you like, for maximum flavor and tenderness it is strongly recommended to cook your non-ground beef and lamb only to medium rare, your non-ground pork to medium, and ground meats to well done.

Another temperature to keep in mind is the temperature of your oven, stove, or grill. Higher heat means your lean grass-fed meats will dry out faster. Except when initially searing meat (see below), you should not go beyond medium when cooking on the stovetop or grill. When slow-cooking larger pieces of meat such as roasts, hams, and racks of ribs, lower the oven or grill temperature called for in your recipe by 50°F.

Tenderization

Because pasture-raised animals actually get to move around, their muscles develop much more than the muscles of confined animals. Unfortunately, well-used muscles translate to tougher cuts of meat, especially as the animal ages. Tenderizing your meat—especially grass-fed beef—before cooking breaks down tough muscle fibers and makes the end result much easier to cut and chew. The best option is a mechanical Jaccard tenderizer. This gadget, sold for approximately $20, contains either 45 or 48 needle-like stainless steel blades that pierce the meat and sever tough muscle fibers. The tool is pressed into the meat like a stamp or stapler and is extremely easy to use and clean. It also helps spices and sauces penetrate deeper into the meat. Marinades are often touted as an option for tenderizing meat, but results are highly dependent on the type of marinade used. Acidic marinades, with ingredients such as lemon or lime juice, vinegar, and wine, can actually dry meat out, rendering it tougher. Marinades that use fruit enzymes (such as those found in papaya, pineapple, and kiwi) to break down the long protein chains in meat's connective tissues are often too powerful, and can quickly turn meat to mush. Dairy-based marinades like those involving buttermilk or yogurt appear to be the most effective, although the exact reason why is not known.

Other Useful Suggestions

The list below provides several additional tips to ensure your culinary success. They are not, however, unique to cooking pasture-raised meat. Rather, they are general best practices that can be used when cooking any cut or type of meat from any source, although the difference they make on grass-fed meat may be more obvious.

- Make sure the meat is completely thawed before cooking. The refrigerator is the best option for defrosting. As mentioned above, smaller packages usually take a day and a half to two days, while larger packages may take up to three and a half days. Even if the meat appears tightly wrapped, place it in a container to catch any potential spills. If you don't have time to defrost in the fridge, thaw the meat in a sink full of cold water. Again, be sure to place the meat in a Ziploc bag or some other watertight container. Never defrost meat in the microwave or on the countertop.

- Regardless of how you'll be cooking it, always begin by searing the meat over high heat on all sides. This sear, technically a combination of the Maillard reaction and the process of caramelization, produces a much richer flavor profile and helps trap moisture inside the meat. Always pat meat dry before searing. The drier the meat, the faster you'll achieve an even, deep brown sear without overcooking the rest of the meat.

- Baste meat while grilling or roasting to keep it moist and flavorful. Butter, a marinade, or pan drippings are all good options.

- Always use tongs or a spatula instead of a fork to turn meat while cooking. Piercing the surface of the meat with the tines of a fork allows valuable juices to escape.

- After cooking, tent meat loosely with foil and allow it to rest to give the juices inside time to cool and redistribute evenly throughout the meat. Smaller items such as steaks and chops should rest for 5 to 10 minutes. Whole chickens and larger cuts like roasts and hams should be rested 15 to 20 minutes. Ground meat (such as burgers and sausages), meat that was sliced or cut before cooking (such as in a stir fry), and meat that will be eaten with the liquid it was cooked in (such as a stew) do not need to rest.

A Note on Offal

Most American consumers shy away from eating, let alone purchasing and cooking, anything that isn't a muscle meat. When asked by the butcher if they want their portion of the available offal, however, most Individuals purchasing a quarter, half, or whole animal will say yes, even if they aren't sure what to do with it. This is a smart move; most offal, especially organ meats, is incredibly nutritious. But actually taking those "weird bits" out of the freezer and doing something with them can feel a bit daunting. Step outside of your comfort zone every few months and create a dish that uses some form of offal. Thankfully, the Internet makes it easy to find recipes and cooking tips for any item you're not sure what to do with.

Bones are probably the most familiar and least intimidating form of offal to work with. Bones can be simmered over low heat for several hours in a soup or stew to add additional flavor. They can be cooked for longer periods of time (16 to 24 hours) to make bone broth, rich in gelatin, amino acids, minerals, and glucosamine, which can either be consumed straight or used as a base in another recipe. Bones, especially smoked ham hocks, can also be used to add flavor to large batches of beans, leafy greens, and other dishes. The marrow from roasted leg bones has a rich, almost sweet, flavor and a buttery texture that many consider a true delicacy.

If you purchased a share of beef or pork, you may have received a package or two of fat. This fat can easily be rendered to produce tallow (beef) or lard (pork). Some butchers may even render and jar the fat for you. Rendering fat is a simple process that involves chopping it up, cooking it over very low heat for several hours, and then straining out the small pieces of meat and gristle from the liquified fat. The resulting product will keep for months in the refrigerator and is excellent for cooking meats, beans, and vegetables. Neutral-flavored leaf lard, rendered from the fat around a pig's kidneys, is also highly prized for the lightness and flakiness it gives to pie crusts, biscuits, and other baked goods. Although lard has gotten a bad rap over the years, new research suggests that this traditional ingredient—once the most commonly used fat in American kitchens—is actually much healthier than butter or hydrogenated vegetable shortening.

Pork skin can be boiled and then fried to produce pork rinds, also known as cracklings. Beef oxtail, chicken and pig feet (trotters), and pig ears are all rendered tender by a long, low simmer.

Which organs you receive will depend on the species and the butcher. If you've purchased lamb or pork, expect to receive all or a portion of the liver, heart, and kidneys. Less commonly, you may also receive sweetbreads—the lamb or pig's thymus gland. Beef shares usually include liver, the heart, and the tongue, but may also include brains, tripe, intestine, and kidneys. Whole chickens, turkeys, and ducks will come with a package of giblets, which includes the heart, gizzard, neck, and liver.

Although many people are familiar with making giblet gravy, there is often a lot of confusion surrounding what to do with other organs. It's helpful to realize that you don't have to re-invent the wheel when preparing organ meats. You can often incorporate organ meats into familiar meals. For example, tacos can be made with chopped, seasoned beef tongue, cubed beef heart can be used in place of stew meat, and chili can be made with a mix of ground meat and ground liver. Many culinary traditions, especially those in Asia, the Middle East, and Latin America, feature delicious recipes where organ meats are the star. Googling "[organ] recipes" will produce a plethora of dish-es to choose from. Some organ meats require a small amount of additional effort, such as removing the outer skin of a beef tongue or removing the center "core" from kidneys, but others, including liver and brains, need no special treatment. Be careful not to overcook organ meats, as this will make them tough and may adversely affect flavor.

Because our palates develop based on the foods we ate growing up, some offal may prove to be an acquired taste. Among organ meats, sweetbreads are widely considered to be the most delicious and least "strange" tasting. They can, however, be a bit tricky to prepare and are less likely to be included in the offal you receive from the butcher. Heart and tongue are very similar in both flavor and texture to "normal" meat (since they, too, are muscles) and are excellent first forays into cooking and eating organs. Brains, which have a mild flavor and a texture similar to scrambled eggs, are another good choice for beginners if your share included them. Pork and beef liver have a strong, metallic flavor and a unique texture that some find off-putting. Lamb and poultry livers are milder in flavor. Kidneys, if not cleaned properly before cooking, can have a very pungent aroma and taste but can be quite mild when prepared correctly.

If you're interested in trying an organ meat but are skeptical that you'll enjoy the taste, look for recipes that include a lot of spices or other strong flavors you enjoy. The Resources section includes a link to a useful primer on cooking the "odd bits," including organs, skin, fat, and bones. If you're really at a loss for what to do with a particular piece of offal (or any cut you've received), the farmer or butcher are usually happy to offer preparation advice and recipes.

Avoiding Burnout

Even with the guidance offered in this book, at some point you may find your enthusiasm for meal planning, cooking at home, and perhaps even meat in general seriously flagging. If deciding on what to make has become drudgery or you feel nauseated at the very sight of a steak, the tips below can help "reset" your motivation and appetite. Even if you aren't struggling, implementing some of these suggestions can make your experience easier and more enjoyable.

- Go meatless (or at least "meat from the freezer"-less) for a week or two. By abstaining from meat (or meat that you have to prepare yourself) for a short period of time, you give both your brain and taste buds a break. You may also want to make it a regular habit to go meatless one or two days each week.

- Make your dishes less meat-centric. If the idea of another "meat and potatoes" meal is starting to turn your stomach, focus on recipes where meat is more of an accent than the main attraction. Many "ethnic" dishes—especially those traditionally eaten by the less affluent classes—depend less on meat and more on vegetables, starches, and spices. And you don't necessarily need to make these dishes with bargain cuts like ground or stew meat; even steaks, pork chops, and other choice cuts can be used.

- Readjust your creativity level. This can work in both directions: If you're bored with eating the same meals week after week, spend some time looking for new recipes. You can explore new cuisines or simply try searching online for recipes that combine a cut you want to use with another ingredient you love. (For example, a search for "pork shoulder mango recipes" turns up several enticing options, including "Caribbean mango pork with tropical rice" and "Kahlua pork sliders with mango blueberry salsa.") Conversely, if you're exhausted from constantly searching for new and different dishes, which may require hard-to-find ingredients or unfamiliar cooking techniques, there's nothing wrong with filling your meal plan with easy-to-make comfort foods for a couple weeks. While eating nothing but meatloaf and grilled bratwurst may throw your pacing "schedule" off a bit, it's well worth the mental break.

- Make use of batch cooking. Just like buying meat in bulk can save you time and effort, cooking in bulk can do the same. Many people swear by this habit, and there are several ways to go about it. The simplest option is to double a recipe you've already planned to make and immediately freeze half of it for a later time. Meals that freeze and reheat well include soups and stews, meatballs, lasagna, casseroles, and braised meats (like short ribs or shanks). Another batching option is to prep (or prep and cook) some or all of your meals for the coming week on one day. These can then be stored in the fridge until needed. The most extreme form of batch cooking involves dedicating one or two days to prepare, cook, and freeze numerous meals. Regardless of the method you choose, cooking in bulk means you'll have readily available options when you don't have the time or energy to meal plan or cook.

- Turn dinner into an occasion. Meal planning and cooking are a lot more fun if it's for a celebration. Consider throwing a dinner party where you provide the main dish and friends or family bring appetizers, sides, drinks, and dessert. This works particularly well with large cuts such as chuck roast, ham, and pork shoulder. If your guests are on the more adventurous side, this is an excellent opportunity to make organ meats such as heart, tongue, or kidneys. (Eating strange foods—even if they don't turn out particularly tasty—is always an entertaining bonding experience.)

- Have someone else do the planning and cooking. If you're typically the one in charge of planning and cooking meals and there's someone in your household you can pass that responsibility off to—even if only for a week or two—do so. While they may not do as good a job as you, the break can help you destress. Another (perhaps better) option is to outsource planning and cooking of several meals to a nearby friend or family member whose culinary talents you admire. You provide the meat, they do the rest, and you split the finished product. This is an especially good option if you have offal you're intimidated by and a particularly adventurous friend or loved one.

If, after trying everything else, you're certain you can't make your bulk meat purchase work for you and your family, you have the options of gifting or selling the meat to family or friends. Depending on the regulations, you may also be able to donate it to a local shelter or food bank. This should of course be a last resort, since you will recoup little, if any, of the initial purchase price.

———

Now that you have a complete, big-picture view of what's involved in finding, buying, storing, and eating such a large quantity of meat, you can take your next steps with confidence. Refer back to these chapters, as well as the appendices and resources, as you go through the meat-buying process—especially the first time around. And while the guidance this book offers will be more than enough to make your experience easy and stress-free, you'll likely discover other tips and tricks as you go along that work particularly well for your unique situation.

QUICK GUIDE TO THE MOST COMMON GRASS-FED AND PASTURE-RAISED ANIMALS

This appendix provides useful information when purchasing the four most common types of meat (beef, pork, lamb, and chicken), including the best breeds and time of year to buy, how much meat you can expect, and common cutting decisions the butcher may ask you to make.

Primals, Their Derivative Cuts, and Cut Instructions

When an animal is butchered, the carcass is first separated into several large pieces of meat called primal cuts. These primals are then divided into various retail cuts, which are packaged for the customer. The number, names, and anatomical locations of primal cuts vary from species to species, and they can also vary from country to country.

In most cases, there are many ways a particular primal can be divided into retail cuts. For example, the beef chuck primal can be divided into roasts (such as arm roast and chuck roast), or it can be turned into steaks (such as flat iron and blade steaks). Or, alternatively, all or part of it could be ground into hamburger or chopped into stew meat. Thus, when a butcher asks for your cut instructions, they are essentially asking how you'd like each primal to be divided up.

In the sections below, you'll find charts showing the primals for each animal, their location on the body, and the most common cuts from that primal. You'll also find lists of the cutting decisions you'll most likely be asked to make. Note, however, that all butchers are different and thus may offer more, fewer, or different cut options than those listed here.

A Note on Seasonality

In the sections below, you'll see that each animal has an optimal time of the year for purchase. While the seasonality of fruits and vegetables is a given, many people are surprised to learn that meat is seasonal as well. After all, industrialized commercial agriculture has made it possible to get any type of meat at any time of year, thanks to keeping animals in highly controlled and heavily modified living conditions. Even small, local farms may harvest their animals throughout the year. But there is actually an ideal time to slaughter beef, pork, lamb, and chicken, based on a combination of the animal's age (which in turn is based on breeding seasons and when babies are born) and the availability and quality of the food it's eaten. Meat from animals slaughtered at the optimal age and time of year will be at peak quality and nutritional value.

Beef

- **Best Breeds:** Angus, Devon, Galloway, Hereford, Highland, Shorthorn, Wagyu
- **Best Time to Buy**: Late summer and early winter
- **Age at Slaughter:** 16–24 months
- **Weight at Slaughter:** 900–1,300 pounds
- **Typical Price Range:** $3.50–$5.50/lb hanging weight

Typical Take-Home Amount:

Share Size	Packaged Meat*	Space Needed	
		Chest Freezer	Upright Freezer
Quarter	90–125 pounds	4–5.5 cu ft	4.5–6 cu ft
Half (Side)	180–250 pounds	8–11 cu ft	9–12 cu ft
Whole	350–500 pounds	16–22 cu ft	18–24 cu ft

* This is meat-only and does not include organs and bones. If you will be including these in your order, allow for additional freezer space.

Primals and Cuts:

Primal	Location	Common Cuts
Chuck	Shoulder, neck, upper arm, and top portion of first five pairs of ribs	Chuck roasts, pot roasts, arm roasts, blade steaks, flat iron steaks
Brisket	Chest/breast	Brisket
Rib	Top portion of sixth through twelfth pairs of ribs	Rib (bone-in) steaks, ribeye (boneless) steaks, rib roasts
Plate	Abdomen below rib primal	Skirt steaks (often used for fajitas), short ribs

Primal	Location	Common Cuts
Loin	Short loin: thirteenth (final) rib to the end of the lumbar spine, extending down to the flank primal Sirloin: directly behind the short loin, the hip extending back to the round primal and down to the flank primal	Short loin: T-bone steaks, strip (NY strip) steaks, beef tenderloin roasts, tenderloin steaks (fillet mignon) Sirloin: top sirloin steaks, sirloin steaks, tri-tip roasts, tri-tip steaks
Flank	Abdomen below loin primal	Flank steaks
Round	Rump and rear thigh	Top round roasts, bottom round roasts, eye of round roasts, rump roasts, sirloin tip steaks, round steaks
Shank	Lower part of the leg	Cross-cut shanks
Trim (scraps) and any unwanted portions will either be ground into hamburger or cut into stew meat. Chuck, brisket, plate, shank, and flank are the primals most often used for hamburger or stew meat.		

Typical Cut Instructions:

- **Number of steaks per package:** 2 or 4
- **Thickness of steaks:** 0.5" to 1.5" (1" is most common)
- **Roast size:** 2–3 lbs or 4–5 lbs
- **Size of hamburger packages:** 1 lb, 1.5 lbs, or 2 lbs (may also offer premade patties)
- **Chuck:** roasts, steaks, or add to trim
- **Brisket:** keep or add to trim
- **Rib:** rib steaks (bone-in), ribeye steaks (boneless), or roasts
- **Plate:** short ribs, steaks, or add to trim
- **Loin:**
  - **Short loin:** T-bone steaks or separate New York strip steaks and filets
  - **Sirloin:** steaks (bone-in or boneless) or roasts

- **Flank:** steaks or add to trim
- **Round:** roasts or steaks (regular or tenderized cube steaks)
- **Shanks:** keep (cross-cut) or add to trim
- **Misc.:** keep or discard heart, tongue, liver, oxtail, and soup bones
- **Specialty products** may include jerky, beef sticks, summer sausage, and beef franks

Sample Order (Quarter Beef):

Cut	Weight per Package	# of Packages	Total Weight
Ground beef	1 lb	33	33 lbs
Chuck roast	4 lbs	2	8 lbs
Arm roast	3 lbs	1	3 lbs
Rump roast	3.5 lbs	1	3.5 lbs
Brisket	4.5 lbs	1	4.5 lbs
Rib steak (2/package)	1.5 lbs	3	4.5 lbs
NY strip steak (2/package)	1.5–2 lbs	3	5 lbs
Tenderloin fillet (2/package)	0.75 lbs	3	2.25 lbs
Sirloin steak (2/package)	1.5 lbs	3	4.5 lbs
Sirloin tip steak (2/package)	1–1.5 lbs	3	4 lbs
Flank steak (2/package)	1.5 lbs	1	1.5 lbs
Cube steak (2/package)	0.75 lbs	6	4.5 lbs
Tri-tip roast	1.75 lbs	1	1.75 lbs
Stew meat	1.5 lbs	6	9 lbs

Cut	Weight per Package	# of Packages	Total Weight
Cross-cut shank	1.25 lbs	2	2.5 lbs
Heart (whole)	2.8 lbs	1	2.8 lbs
Tongue (whole)	1.5 lbs	1	1.5 lbs
Liver (quarter)	0.75 lbs	2	1.5 lbs
Bones	16 lbs	1	16 lbs
		Meat-Only Total	91.5 lbs
		Total	113.3 lbs

Pork

- **Best Breeds:** Berkshire, Duroc, Gloucestershire Old Spot, Old Black, Red Wattle, Tamworth
- **Best Time to Buy:** fall and winter
- **Age at Slaughter:** 6 months
- **Weight at Slaughter:** 250–350 pounds
- **Typical Price Range:** $4.50–$6.50/lb hanging weight

Typical Take-Home Amount:

Share Size	Packaged Meat*	Space Needed	
		Chest Freezer	Upright Freezer
Half (Side)	65–85 pounds	3–4 cu ft	3.5–4.5 cu ft
Whole	130–170 pounds	6–8 cu ft	7–9 cu ft

* This is meat-only and does not include organs and bones. If you will be including these in your order, allow for additional freezer space.

Primals and Cuts:

Primal	Location	Common Cuts
Jowl	Cheek	Cured jowl bacon (slab or sliced)
Shoulder (butt or Boston butt)	Butt or Boston butt: upper shoulder and neck Picnic or picnic ham: lower shoulder and upper arm	Pork shoulder roasts, pork butt roasts, shoulder steaks

Primal	Location	Common Cuts
Loin	Top portion of the animal, between front and back legs, includes rib, center loin, and sirloin	Rib chops, loin chops, baby back ribs, country-style ribs, blade roasts, center-cut roasts, tenderloin roasts, sirloin roasts
Belly	Underside of the animal, including lower portion of ribs and abdomen	Spareribs, fresh pork belly, bacon (slab or sliced)
Leg (Ham)	Rump and rear leg	Hams (fresh or cured), ham steaks
Hock	Lower part of the leg	Smoked or fresh hocks
Trim (scraps) and any unwanted portions will be ground into sausage. Pork shoulder is the primal most often used for sausage.		

Typical Cut Instructions:

- **Number of chops per package:** 2 or 4
- **Thickness of chops:** 0.5" to 1.5" (1" is most common)
- **Jowl:** smoked (sliced or left as slab), uncured, or add to trim
- **Shoulder:** roasts (boneless or bone-in), steaks, or add to trim
- **Loin:** rib and loin chops (bone-in or boneless) or roasts; if you want baby back ribs and tenderloin you must select boneless chops/roasts
- **Belly:** cured bacon (sliced or left as slab) or fresh pork belly
- **Spareribs:** keep or add to trim
- **Ham:** hams (fresh or cured, whole or halved) or ham steaks
- **Hocks:** smoked, fresh, or add to trim
- **Trim:** ground (no seasoning) or various sausage flavors (breakfast, sage, chorizo, sweet Italian, hot Italian, kielbasa, bratwurst, etc.); links, patties, or loose
- **Misc.:** keep or discard liver, kidneys, heart, skin, fat, feet, ears, and soup bones

Sample Order (Half Hog):

Cut	Weight per Package	# of Packages	Total Weight
Shoulder roast	3–3.5 lbs	5	17 lbs
Loin chops (2/ package)	1.75 lbs	5	8.75 lbs
Rib chops (2/ package)	1.75 lbs	5	8.75 lbs
Spareribs (1 rack/ package)	1.8 lbs	1	1.8 lbs
Ground pork	1 lb	8	8 lbs
Italian sausage (4/ package)	1 lb	8	8 lbs
Bacon (approx. 12 slices/package)	1 lb	8	8 lbs
Jowl bacon (approx. 6-12 slices/ package)	0.6–1 lbs	2	1.6 lbs
Bacon ends and pieces	0.5 lbs	1	0.5 lbs
Sweetheart ham (cured)	1 lb	2	2 lbs
Ham (cured)	4.5 lbs	2	9 lbs
Ham hock (cured)	2 lbs	2	4 lbs
Fat	0.8–1.3 lbs	2	2.1 lbs
Skin	1.2–2.4 lbs	4	7 lbs
Liver (half)	1.3 lbs	1	1.3 lbs
Heart (half)	0.3 lbs	1	0.3 lbs
Kidney (single)	0.3 lbs	1	0.3 lbs
Bones	4.4 lbs	1	4.4 lbs
		Meat-Only Total	77.4 lbs
		Total	92.8 lbs

Lamb

- **Best Breeds:** Black Bellied Barbados, Dorper, Dorset, Katahdin, Suffolk, Targhee, Tunis
- **Best Time to Buy:** spring and fall
- **Age at Slaughter:** 6–8 months
- **Weight at Slaughter:** 100–125 pounds
- **Typical Price Range:** $6.00–$8.00/lb hanging weight

Typical Take-Home Amount:

Share Size	Packaged Meat*	Space Needed	
		Chest Freezer	Upright Freezer
Half (Side)	18–22 pounds	0.75–1 cu ft	1–1.25 cu ft
Whole	36–44 pounds	1.5–2 cu ft	2–2.5 cu ft

* This is meat-only and does not include organs and bones. If you will be including these in your order, allow for additional freezer space.

Primals and Cuts:

Primal	Location	Common Cuts
Neck	Neck	Neck roasts
Shoulder	Shoulder	Shoulder roasts, shoulder chops
Breast	Chest	Breast roasts, spareribs
Rib	Top portion of sixth through twelfth pairs of ribs	Rack of lamb, rib chops

Primal	Location	Common Cuts
Loin	Top portion of the animal's back from the final pair of ribs to the hipbone	Loin roasts, loin chops
Flank	Abdomen below loin primal	Flank roasts, flank steaks
Leg	Rear legs	bone-in or boneless leg roasts
Shank	Lower part of the leg	Shanks
Trim (scraps) and any unwanted portions will be ground or cut into stew meat. Lamb neck, breast, and flank primals are most commonly used for ground lamb or stew meat.		

Typical Cut Instructions:

- **Number of chops per package:** 2 or 4
- **Neck:** roasts or add to trim
- **Shoulder:** roasts or steaks
- **Breast:** roasts or add to trim
- **Spareribs:** keep or add to trim
- **Rib:** rack of lamb or rib chops
- **Loin:** roasts or chops
- **Flank:** roasts, steaks, or add to trim
- **Leg:** bone-in (whole) roasts, boneless (half) roasts, or steaks
- **Shank:** keep or add to trim
- **Misc.:** keep or discard liver, heart, kidneys, and soup bones

Sample Order (Whole Lamb):

Cut	Weight per Package	# of Packages	Total Weight
Rib chops (4/package)	1 lb	4	4 lbs
Loin chops (4/package)	1.5 lbs	4	6 lbs
Spareribs (1 rack/package)	1.25 lbs	2	2.5 lbs
Leg of lamb	3.5 lbs	4	14 lbs
Ground lamb	1 lb	5	5 lbs
Stew meat	1.5 lbs	5	7.5 lbs
Shanks	2 lbs	2	4 lbs
Heart, liver, and kidneys	3 lbs	1	3 lbs
Bones	2–4 lbs	2	6 lbs
		Meat-Only Total	43 lbs
		Total	52 lbs

Chicken

- **Best Breeds:** Barred Plymouth Rock, Bresse, Cornish Cross, Freedom Ranger, Jersey Giant, Orpington
- **Best Time to Buy:** Late spring and summer
- **Age at Slaughter:** 7–14 weeks, depending on breed and desired size
- **Weight at Slaughter:** 4–8 pounds
- **Typical Price Range:** $3.50–$5.50/lb hanging weight

Typical Take-Home Amount:

Most processed chickens weigh between 3 and 7 pounds (including the bones). You should be able to fit 2 to 3 birds per cubic foot of freezer space in either a chest freezer or upright freezer.

Primals and Cuts:

Chickens are usually sold as whole birds. However, some butchers may break these down into "primals" of breast, wing, and either thighs and legs (drumsticks) or leg quarters (thigh and drumstick connected).

Typical Cut Instructions:

Some butchers offer customers the option of having the whole bird divided into its various parts. If this is the case, you may be asked some or all of the following:

- **Breasts:** skin-on or skinless

- **Leg quarters:** keep together or divide into separate packages of thighs and drumsticks
- **Thighs:** skin-on or skinless, bone-in or boneless
- **Misc.:** giblets (gizzard, liver, heart, and neck), feet

APPENDIX B

COOKING GRASS-FED AND PASTURE-RAISED MEAT

This appendix offers some basic guidelines for cooking grass-fed and pasture-raised meat, including the basic characteristics of and best cooking practices for the various primals and their derivative cuts, as well as information on measuring doneness using internal temperature, color, and texture.

Tough vs. Tender, Moist vs. Dry Heat

At the most basic level, all you need to know to cook a piece of meat successfully is whether you should use quick, dry heat or slow, moist heat. This decision is dictated by the characteristics of the cut—specifically, how tough or tender it is.

Knowing which primal (part of the body) the cut comes from will reveal how you should cook it. The various retail cuts from a single primal tend to share the same general characteristics in terms of tenderness, fattiness, and flavor because they all come from the same part of the animal. Generally, the cuts that come from the center of the animal (such as the rib and loin areas) are the most tender because these muscles don't do much work. The parts of the animal that are frequently exercised, such as the shoulders and the legs, have more connective tissue and, thus, are tougher. Flavor preferences can be quite subjective, but, for most people, the more intramuscular fat (marbling) a cut has, the more flavorful it will taste.

Tough cuts should be cooked using slow, moist heat. All moist heat methods involve some form of moisture, whether that's steam, water, broth, wine, or some other liquid. Examples include stewing, braising, steaming, poaching, boiling, and slow-roasting in an oven or crockpot (where steam builds up as the meat slowly cooks). Smokers may utilize either moist or dry heat but, because of their "low and slow" nature are best suited to tougher cuts of meat such as brisket and pork shoulder. For moist heat methods to be successful, cooking temperatures must be kept relatively low (at or below 212° F) and the meat is cooked for a long time. The moisture and long cooking time allow the tightly-knit muscle fibers to "unwind," rendering the once-tough cut quite tender. Collagen in the connective tissue breaks down into gelatin, which prevents the meat from becoming dry and tough once more.

Tender cuts of meat should be cooked with quick, dry heat. Dry heat methods do not use any moisture and instead transfer heat to the meat via heated air, hot metal, or some other medium. (Because fats and oils repel water, they do not have the same characteristics as the liquids used in moist heat methods. So even though cooking oils and fats liquify at high heat, using them is still considered dry heat cooking.) Examples include grilling, pan- and deep-frying, sautéing, broiling, and high-temperature roasting in an oven. Cooking temperatures are much hotter (above 300° F) and the meat is cooked for a much shorter time. It is important to note that the browning of meat (known as the Maillard reaction) can only happen using dry heat cooking (and only when the meat itself is free of surface moisture). This is why many recipes that use moist heat methods call for an initial searing of the meat using dry heat.

If you were to cook a tough cut of meat using quick, dry heat, the meat would remain quite tough and chewy because the tough muscle fibers and connective tissue wouldn't have had time to break down. Interestingly, if you cooked a tender cut of meat with slow, moist heat, it would also likely turn out tough, because there isn't enough collagen to protect the meat during the long cooking time.

Some cuts of meat, like flank steaks, straddle the line between tough and tender and can be cooked using either quick, dry heat or slow, moist heat. In cases like these, marinating the meat before using a quick, dry cooking method like grilling can help tenderize the meat. Cutting the meat into small pieces and stir-frying also works well for these "borderline" cuts because it manually breaks down tough muscle fibers.

Primal	Common Cuts	Characteristics	Best Cooking Methods
Beef			
Chuck	Chuck roast, pot roast, arm roast, blade steaks, flat iron steaks	Moderately tough with lots of connective tissue, moderately lean, moderately flavorful	Slow, moist heat (braise, slow-roast) for roasts; quick, dry heat (stir-fry, marinate and grill) for steaks
Brisket	Brisket	Moderately tough with long and thick muscle fibers, very fatty, very flavorful	Slow, moist heat (braise, slow-roast) or smoke
Rib	Rib (bone-in) steaks, ribeye (boneless) steaks, rib roast	Moderately tender, well-marbled, very flavorful	Quick, dry heat (grill, pan fry, broil)
Plate	Skirt steak (often used for fajitas), short ribs	Moderately tough with lots of connective tissue, moderately fatty, moderately flavorful	Quick, dry heat (stir fry, marinate and grill) for steaks; slow, moist heat (braise, slow-roast) for short ribs
Loin	Short loin: T-bone steaks, strip (NY strip) steaks, beef tenderloin roasts, tenderloin steaks (fillet mignon) Sirloin: top sirloin steaks, sirloin steaks, tri-tip roasts, tri-tip steaks	Very tender, moderately lean, very flavorful (the sirloin is less tender but more flavorful than the short loin)	Quick, dry heat (grill, pan fry, broil, high-temperature roast)

Primal	Common Cuts	Characteristics	Best Cooking Methods
Flank	Flank steak	Very tough, very lean, very flavorful	Quick, dry heat (stir fry, marinate and grill) or slow, moist heat (braise)
Round	Top round, bottom round, eye of round, and rump roasts; sirloin tip steaks, round steaks	Moderately tough, very lean, moderately flavorful	Slow, moist heat (braise, slow-roast) for roasts; quick, dry heat (stir fry, marinate and grill, broil) for steaks
Shank	Cross-cut shanks	Very tough, moderately fatty, moderately flavorful	Slow, moist heat (braise, slow-roast, stew)
Pork			
Jowl	Cured jowl bacon (slab or sliced)	Moderately tender, very fatty, very flavorful	quick, dry heat (pan fry)
Shoulder (butt or Boston butt)	Pork shoulder roast, pork butt roast	Moderately tough with lots of connective tissue, moderately fatty, very flavorful	Slow, moist heat (braise, slow-roast) or smoke
Loin	Rib chops, loin chops, baby back ribs, country-style ribs, blade roast, center-cut roast, tenderloin roast, sirloin roast	Very tender, moderately lean, moderately flavorful	Quick, dry heat (grill, pan fry, high-temperature roast)

Primal	Common Cuts	Characteristics	Best Cooking Methods
Belly	Spareribs, fresh pork belly, bacon (slab or sliced)	Moderately tender, very fatty, very flavorful	Slow, moist heat (braise, slow-roast) or smoke spareribs; quick, dry heat (pan fry) for bacon and pork belly
Leg (Ham)	Ham (fresh or cured), ham steaks	Moderately tender, very lean, moderately flavorful	Slow, moist heat (low-temperature roast) for hams; quick, dry heat (pan fry) for ham steaks
Hock	Smoked or fresh hocks	Very tough, moderately fatty, moderately flavorful	Slow, moist heat (braise, slow-roast, stew)
Lamb			
Neck	Neck roasts	Very tough, moderately lean, moderately flavorful	Slow, moist heat (braise, slow-roast)
Shoulder	Shoulder roasts, shoulder chops	Moderately tender, moderately lean, moderately flavorful	Slow, moist heat (braise, slow-roast) for roasts; quick, dry heat (grill, pan fry) for chops
Breast	Breast roasts, spareribs	Very tough, moderately lean, moderately flavorful	Slow, moist heat (braise, slow-roast)
Rib	Rack of lamb, rib chops	Very tender, well marbled, very flavorful	Quick, dry heat (grill, pan fry, high-temperature roast)
Loin	Loin roast, loin chops	Very tender, moderately lean, moderately flavorful	Quick, dry heat (grill, pan fry, high-temperature roast)

Primal	Common Cuts	Characteristics	Best Cooking Methods
Flank	Flank roasts, flank steaks	Very tough, moderately fatty, moderately flavorful	Slow, moist heat (braise, slow-roast) for roasts; quick, dry heat (stir fry, marinate and grill) or slow, moist heat (braise) for steaks
Leg	Whole (bone-in) or boneless leg roasts	Moderately tender, very lean, very flavorful	Slow, moist heat (braise, slow-roast)
Shank	Shanks	Very tough, moderately fatty, moderately flavorful	Slow, moist heat (braise, slow-roast, stew)
Chicken			
Whole chickens and chicken parts can be cooked using either quick, dry heat or slow, moist heat			
Trim - Ground Meat (Beef, Pork, Lamb, and Chicken)			
Ground meat, including sausage, can be cooked using either quick, dry heat or slow, moist heat			

Gauging Doneness

Since grass-fed and, to a lesser extent, pasture-raised meats may cook faster than conventional meats because of their lower fat content, it's best to go by internal temperature rather than time when cooking. With more cooking experience, it becomes easy to tell when meat is done based on color, texture, and firmness, but if you're in doubt, use an instant read thermometer and the chart below.

Meat	Internal Temperature[1]	Rest Time[2]	Characteristics
Beef and Lamb			
Steaks, Chops, and Leg of Lamb	125° F (rare) 135° F (medium-rare) 145° F (medium) 155° F (medium-well) 160°+ F (well)	5 minutes	Rare: bright red, warm center and pinkish elsewhere; soft to the touch Medium-rare: very pink, slightly hot center and beginning to brown elsewhere; beginning to firm up Medium: pale pink center and brown elsewhere; slightly firm to the touch Medium-well: only slightly pink in the center and gray/brown elsewhere; firm to the touch Well: uniformly gray/brown; hard to the touch
Roasts and Brisket	180° F[3]	10 minutes	Meat should pull apart easily
Ground	160° F	None	No pink visible
Pork			
Chops and Tenderloin	145° F (medium) 160° F (well)	5 minutes	Medium: pale pink center; slightly firm to the touch Well: uniformly white/tan; hard to the touch
Shoulder	180° F	10 minutes	Meat should pull apart easily
Ham (Smoked)	145° F	10 minutes	Because the ham is cured, you are technically just heating it up
Ham (Fresh)	160° F	10 minutes	Meat yields easily to a fork and begins to separate from the bone

Meat	Internal Temperature[1]	Rest Time[2]	Characteristics
Ground and Sausage	160° F	None	No pink visible
Ribs	180° F	None	White to tan; meat should come away easily from the bone
Chicken			
Whole and parts	165° F	5 minutes	Juices should run clear
Ground	165° F	None	No pink visible

1. To ensure proper food safety, the USDA recommends that pork, beef, and lamb be cooked to at least medium and that chicken be cooked to well done. In the case of beef and lamb, however, many people enjoy their steaks/chops rare or medium-rare. When cooking grass-fed beef and lamb, most people find that anything cooked beyond medium will be very dry and tough.

2. Because meat will continue to cook as it rests, you should remove steaks/chops from heat when they are 5° F below desired internal temperature and larger pieces of meat such as roasts and hams when they are 10° F below desired internal temperature. Because they are not rested after cooking, ground meat and ribs should be cooked until they reach the desired internal temperature.

3. Cooking cuts with a significant amount of tough connective tissue to an internal temperature of 180° F ensures that the collagen fibers will be broken down, rendering the meat tender.

APPENDIX C
TEMPLATES

In this appendix you'll find several blank templates that will help you stay organized as you buy, store, and eat your bulk meat purchase. Feel free to print or copy each one for your own use, making any necessary changes to meet your individual circumstances. Each template also includes a sample so that you can see what a filled-out version might look like.

- Farmer Comparison Chart
- Basic Freezer Inventory
- Weekly Meal Plan

Farmer Comparison Chart

Meat Type and Share Size:						
	Farm					
	Butcher					
Criteria	#1:					
	#2:					
	#3:					
	#4:					
	Notes					

Sample:

Meat Type and Share Size: *Quarter Beef*						
	Farm	[name, address, phone number, and website omitted for anonymity]	[name, address, phone number, and website omitted for anonymity]	[name, address, phone number, and website omitted for anonymity]	[name, address, phone number, and website omitted for anonymity]°	[name, address, phone number, and website omitted for anonymity]
	Butcher	[name, address, phone number, and website omitted for anonymity]	[name, address, phone number, and website omitted for anonymity]	[name, address, phone number, and website omitted for anonymity]	[name, address, phone number, and website omitted for anonymity]	?
Criteria	#1: Availability	Ready in late August	?	Ready in early September	Ready in late August and early January	Ready in July
	#2: Price	$3.75/lb + $20 slaughter fee and $0.50/lb processing fee	$4.50/lb (including butcher fees)	$5.25/lb (including butcher fees)	$3.50/lb + butcher fees	$4.00/lb + $100 flat butcher fee
	#3: Type of packaging	?	Freezer paper	Vacuum-sealed plastic	?	?
	#4: Sample before buying?	No	Can buy individual cuts at farmers market	No	Can buy a 10-lb sample box for $115	No
	Notes	Get packaging info from butcher $50 off if ordered by end of May	Email to find out availability	Spoke with John on 5/27	Get fee and packaging info from butcher	Emailed farm 5/25 to find out which butcher they use

Basic Freezer Inventory

Cut	Weight per Package	Number of Packages	Packages Used	Pounds Eaten This Month

Sample:

Cut	Weight per Package	Number of Packages	Packages Used	Pounds Eaten This Month
Beef				
Sirloin steak (2)	1.5 lbs	3	1	
Ground beef	1 lb	30	17	1
Stew meat	1.5 lbs	6	2	3
Rump roast	3.5 lbs	1		
Liver (sliced)	0.75 lbs	3	2	0.75
Pork				
Ham	3.5 / 4.5 lbs	2	1	4.5
Italian sausage (4 links)	1 lb	8	2	1
Bacon (approx. 10 slices)	1 lb	10	4	
Rib chops (2)	1.75 lbs	6	1	1.75
Chicken				
Whole fryer	4–5.5 lbs	4	2	5
Misc.				
Burger buns (8)	10 oz	2	1	
Homemade beef bone broth	1 cup	16	5	1

Weekly Meal Plan

Day	Breakfast	Lunch	Dinner	Prep

Sample:

Day	Breakfast	Lunch	Dinner	Prep
Sunday	Brunch out w/ friends	Salad	Tofu & veggie stir-fry	Make big batch of minestrone soup
Monday	Oatmeal	Sandwich & minestrone	Chorizo-stuffed peppers	Go grocery shopping
Tuesday	Smoothie	Sandwich & minestrone	Order pizza (Little League game)	Take out ground beef for meatballs
Wednesday	Oatmeal	Catered team lunch at work	Leftover chorizo-stuffed peppers	Take out lamb kabob meat
Thursday	Smoothie	Sandwich & minestrone	Spaghetti & meatballs	Start marinating lamb Take out bacon Take out chicken
Friday	Bagel Friday at work	Leftover spaghetti & meatballs	Moroccan lamb & veggie kabobs	Go to farmers market
Saturday	Bacon/eggs/ toast	Sandwich & salad	Date night dinner out	-
Sunday	Bacon/eggs/ toast	Try new Thai food truck	Roast chicken w/ potatoes & broccoli	Shred leftover chicken
Monday	Oatmeal	Sandwich & salad	Chicken tacos	Go grocery shopping

GLOSSARY

Automatic Defrost Freezer – A type of freezer that periodically raises the temperature within the freezer compartment to just above freezing, allowing any accumulated frost to melt and drain to an external tray where it evaporates. These freezers are also known as frost-free or self-defrosting freezers.

Boxed Weight – See Cut and Wrap Weight.

CAFO – Concentrated animal feeding operation, also commonly referred to as a feedlot. The USDA defines CAFOs as farms where at least 1,000 "animal units" are raised in confinement for more than 45 days of the year. An "animal unit" is defined as 1,000 pounds of live weight, and 1,000 "animal units" is equal to 1,000 beef cattle, 2,500 hogs, or 125,000 broiler chickens.

Carcass Weight – See Hanging Weight.

Chest Freezer – A standalone freezer with a lid that opens upward from the top of the unit. Compared to an upright freezer, chest freezers have a much larger footprint and little if any built-in organization, but are more efficient and cost-effective. All chest freezers are manual defrost freezers.

CLA – Conjugated linoleic acid. A type of omega-6 fatty acid found in meat and dairy products derived from ruminants, and found in higher quantities in grass-fed ruminants. CLA is believed to have a number of health benefits, including promoting weight loss and preventing cancer, although more research is needed.

CSA – Community-supported agriculture. A model of agriculture in which customers buy shares of a farm's harvest. Although shares are usually paid for in one lump sum, CSA members typically receive products on a weekly or monthly basis.

Custom-Exempt – A butcher that is not required to undergo continuous inspection by federal or state agencies because it processes meat only for the owner(s) of an animal. This does not mean, however, that custom-exempt butchers are not inspected regularly.

Cut and Wrap Weight – The total weight of the individually wrapped packages a customer takes home after an animal has been processed by a butcher.

Dressed Weight – See Hanging Weight.

Dressing Percentage – The percent difference between an animal's live weight and its hanging weight.

Final Weight – See Cut and Wrap Weight.

Food Miles – The total distance a food item travels during the course of its production, processing, and distribution for sale.

Hanging Weight – The weight of an animal after slaughter, once the head, feet, hide, blood, and internal organs have been removed. When buying meat in bulk, per-pound prices are almost always based on an animal's hanging weight.

Heritage Breeds – Traditional livestock breeds raised before the advent of centralized, industrialized agriculture. Also known as heirloom breeds, heritage breeds tend to be slower-growing and hardier than breeds used in industrialized agriculture.

Industrialized Agriculture – The raising of food (both animal- and plant-based) in large, highly centralized farming operations. Industrial agriculture relies heavily on scientific innovation and focuses on maximizing yields. This is the most common form of agriculture practiced in the United States today, and concerned consumers argue that it has many negative economic, environmental, political, and social consequences.

Kill Fee – The fee charged by a butcher for slaughtering an animal, transporting it to be processed (if applicable), and properly disposing of its remains.

Live Weight – The weight of an animal immediately before it is slaughtered.

Manual Defrost Freezer – A type of freezer in which accumulated frost must be removed by hand, either by scraping it from the interior sides of the freezer or by unplugging the empty freezer and allowing the frost to melt and then drain through a hole at the bottom of the freezer.

Mixed Quarter – A quarter share of an animal (usually a steer) that contains a roughly equal distribution of cuts from both the front and the rear of the animal.

Offal – The internal organs of an animal eaten as food. In a more general sense, the term offal may also be used to refer to other edible parts of an animal that are neither muscle no organs, such as blood, oxtail, skin, etc.

Pastured or Pasture-Raised – An animal that is raised chiefly or entirely outside on pastureland. It is important to note that "pastured" is not necessarily the same as "grass-fed." Pastured hogs and chickens are usually still given supplemental feed. The use of this term is not regulated by the USDA.

Percentage Yield – The percent difference between an animal's hanging weight and its cut and wrap weight.

Primal – A large piece of meat initially separated from the carcass of an animal during butchering that is then broken down into sub-primal and retail cuts.

Processing Fee – The per-pound fee charged by a butcher for cutting, trimming, packaging, and labeling meat from a slaughtered animal. Additional services, such as curing, seasoning, and tenderizing, may or may not be included in the standard processing fee.

Ruminants – Any animal species, including cattle and sheep, that uses fermentation to break down plant material for sustenance. Ruminants' multi-chambered stomachs are designed to digest grasses and do not handle corn and other grains well.

Share (of Beef, Pork, Etc.) – The percentage of an animal a customer agrees to buy from a farmer. Technically, when someone buys a share, they are purchasing partial ownership of the live animal, rather than purchasing the meat itself.

Side (of Beef, Pork, Etc.) – Half of an animal; all the cuts from either the left or right side of the animal.

Slaughter Fee – See Kill Fee.

Split Half – See Mixed Quarter.

Take-Home Weight – See Cut and Wrap Weight.

Upright Freezer – A standalone freezer with a door that opens out from the front of the unit. Compared to a chest freezer, upright freezers have a much narrower footprint and are easier to organize, but are less efficient and often more expensive. Upright freezers can be either manual defrost or automatic defrost freezers.

Weight on the Hoof – See Live Weight.

RESOURCES

Animal Welfare Certifications

5-Step Animal Welfare Program by Global Animal Partnership
https://globalanimalpartnership.org/shoppers/

Certified Animal Welfare Approved by A Greener World
https://agreenerworld.org/certifications/animal-welfare-approved/

Certified Humane by Humane Farm Animal Care
https://certifiedhumane.org/

Freezers

Consumer Reports Freezer Ratings
https://www.consumerreports.org/products/freezer/ratings-overview/

Energy Star Freezer Ratings
https://www.energystar.gov/productfinder/product/certified-residential-freezers/

Kill A Watt EZ Electricity Usage Monitor
https://www.amazon.com/P3-International-P4460-
Electricity-Monitor/dp/B000RGF29Q/ref=sr_1_3?ie=UTF8&
qid=1544845155&sr=8-3&keywords=Kill+A+Watt+EZ+Elec
tricity+Usage+Monitor

Lodge Pan Scrapers (for preventing frost buildup)
https://www.amazon.com/Lodge-Scrapers-Handheld-
Polycarbonate-Cleaners/dp/B0039UU9UO/re
f=sr_1_3?ie=UTF8&qid=1544845223&sr=8-
3&keywords=lodge+pan+scraper

Farm Directories

Eatwild Farm Directory
http://www.eatwild.com/products/index.html

LocalHarvest Farms Directory
https://www.localharvest.org/organic-farms/

Preparing and Cooking Grass-Fed and Pasture-Raised Meat

Basic Beef, Pork, and Lamb Primal Cuts
https://www.thespruceeats.com/cuts-of-meat-beef-pork-
lamb-995843

Directory of Beef Cuts (by primal, cooking method, and occasion)

https://www.beefitswhatsfordinner.com/cuts

A Beginners' Guide to Cooking Odd Bits (With Recipes You
Already Know)
https://paleoleap.com/cooking-organ-meat/

Making Fresh Bone Stock
https://paleoleap.com/making-fresh-bone-stock/

Jaccard 48-Blade Meat Tenderizer
https://www.amazon.com/Jaccard-200348-
Supertendermatic-48-Blade-Tenderizer/
dp/B001347JK6/ref=sr_1_4?s=home-
garden&ie=UTF8&qid=1544846548&sr=1-
4&keywords=jaccard+meat+tenderizer

ThermoPro Digital Instant Read Probe Thermometer
https://www.amazon.com/ThermoPro-TP-16-
Thermometer-Stainless-Standard/dp/B017613C3C/ref
=sr_1_5?s=kitchen&ie=UTF8&qid=1544846450&sr=1-
5&keywords=probe+thermometer

ABOUT THE AUTHOR

Maxine Taylor is a health and wellness acquisitions editor, freelance content developer, and lover of all things tasty. Since making her first purchases in 2011, she's become an outspoken champion of the "whole animal" way of buying and enjoying local, humanely raised meat.

Her goal is to show everyone how easy and rewarding this traditional way of eating can be. She holds degrees in literature, history, and professional writing from the University of California, Santa Barbara, and is a certified technical writer and instructional designer. Maxine currently lives in Portland, Oregon.